The Moral Purposes of
Social Work

The Nelson-Hall Series in Social Welfare
Consulting Editor: Charles Zastrow
University of Wisconsin-Whitewater

The Moral Purposes of Social Work

The Character and Intentions of a Profession

Editors

P. Nelson Reid
North Carolina State University

and

Philip R. Popple
Auburn University

Nelson-Hall Publishers
Chicago

Project Editor: Sheila Whalen
Cover Painting: *View to the Sky* by Henry Maron

Library of Congress Cataloging-in-Publication Data

The Moral purposes of social work : the character and intentions of a
    profession / edited by P. Nelson Reid and Philip R. Popple.
        p. cm.
    ISBN 0-8304-1246-8
    1. Social service—Moral and ethical aspects. 2. Social workers—
Professional ethics—United States.   I. Reid, P. Nelson.
II. Popple, Philip R.
HV10.5.M67   1992
361.3′2—dc20   91-36328
                                                                          CIP

Manufactured in the United States of America

10   9   8   7   6   5   4   3   2   1

∞ ™ The paper used in this book meets the
minimum requirements of American
National Standard for Information
Sciences—Permanence of Paper for
Printed Library Materials, ANSI
Z39.48-1984.

Contents

v

Contents

Contents

CHAPTER EIGHT

Social Work: Social Function and Moral Purpose   141

Philip R. Popple

CHAPTER NINE

Moral Goodness and Black Women: Late Nineteenth Century Community Caregivers   155

Wilma Peebles-Wilkins and Beverly Koerin

CHAPTER TEN

Responding to the Call   173

Maria O'Neil McMahon

About the Contributors   189

Index   193

Preface

One of the unfortunate developments of late twentieth century culture has been a decline in the use of the language and concepts of morality. These concepts, sacred or secular, have been replaced and diminished by the inherently relativistic notion of "values" or the construct of "ethics" applied to particular social situations. The more inclusive and absolutist language of morality, especially in the context of social problems and policy, has become the nearly exclusive province of political conservatism.

This is unfortunate for a number of reasons. First of all social work and, indeed, the related "policy sciences", once used the language of public and private morality as a basis for their existence. Such language was widely and eloquently used by both the right and the left. Secondly, moral rationale and reasoning are very much part of our culture and to have only one side of our political and public philosophical life speaking in moral terms is to have something of an imbalance—which may well be relevant to the popular success of political conservatism in recent U.S. history. This book is in part an effort to explore the meaning of morality in current social work and to recapture an entire area of discourse.

A concern with the decline in discourse related to morality in our profession led to the conduct, in the spring of 1988, of a symposium at North Carolina State University under the title *The Moral Purposes of Social Work*. The keynote was provided by Frederic Reamer, whose thoughtful and substantive address exhorted us all to redouble our commitment to the poor and to public social services in the name of the original and finest aspect of social work's moral intentions. Several of the contributors to this volume were members of that panel, and we decided, shortly thereafter, to expand the discussion and put it in book form.

The symposium was sponsored by North Carolina State University's Ellen Winston Lecture and Development Fund in Social Work. Dr. Winston was, among many other things, U.S. Commissioner of Welfare in the Department of Health, Education, and Welfare in the 1960s and made a distinguished contribution to the development of public assistance and public social programs in North Carolina and throughout the nation. No one could embody the commitment to public social welfare more thoroughly than Dr. Winston. Any reflection on her life and work necessarily poses the questions of what social work is all about and of its relation to both public services and the public interest.

Social work 'as a profession has undergone a number of changes in the twentieth century, many of them reflecting both material changes in our society and shifts in our ideas about people, society, and government. The early twentieth century was fertile ground for the development and expansion of broad governmental responsibility for social problems and for the optimistic vision that through political will, effective service, and adequate income supports, we could tackle and solve a myriad social difficulties. The idea of the welfare state and of the centrality of government and public service seemed both inevitable and ultimately invincible. Social work born of "scientific charity" and christened in American progressivism reflected both a boundless optimism and an easy acceptance of state responsibility for society and its people. Dr. Winston would have understood all these and contributed mightily to their implementation.

But the latter part of the twentieth century has been less kind to both liberal optimism and the concept of the welfare state. In this country and others we have lost our political zeal and the conviction that problems can be fixed through public processes and public action. We are likely today to see the pitfalls of big government and to worry about tax burdens and disincentives. Rather than grand public commitment, we see bureaucracy and worry that it is wasteful and ineffective, constraining innovation and unresponsive to those it serves. Ideas of limited government, volunteerism, and privatization are in vogue and seem not some passing fancy but the wave of the foreseeable future.

Social work has experienced this change and has adapted as best it can to changing realities. The old paradigm is gone, the old rational seems less relevant, the public context (and budget!) has changed, and we look for something that gives our work renewed meaning and direction. The profession feels itself under seige from the political right and is struggling to find an effective defense. Scientific research into practice techniques has given us much useful information but has proven impotent as a defense against our critics. We must roll up our sleeves, enter the fray, and argue for social work's existence, expansion, and utility on normative as well as empirical grounds. This is the purpose of this book.

Acknowledgments

Special thanks are due our contributors. The editors have had the entirely enjoyable task of working with a group that without exception produced substantive manuscripts and produced them on time. Each contributor responded to the original task with zeal and to the subsequent requests of the editors with both speed and diligence. We have never worked with a more able or task-oriented group, and if there were delays in contributions or in the process of putting this all together, those delays were caused by the editors themselves.

We thank our colleagues at North Carolina State University and Auburn University. At North Carolina State the support of the Winston Fund was essential. Special thanks go to Professor Jeffrey Obler (University of North Carolina at Chapel Hill), a member of the original panel, whose thoughtful remarks at the symposium and whose later comments on some of the chapters were invaluable. Thanks to the students in Reid's social policy class in the Spring of 1988 in the graduate school of social work at Chapel Hill and to the undergraduates in the special "moral purposes" seminar held in the fall of 1990 at North Carolina State. Students in both groups argued over the merits, and especially the demerits, or utilitarianism and many of the other concepts in these papers. In so doing they both sharpened and enriched the project.

We wish to gratefully acknowledge the support, encouragement, and help of Steve Ferrara, president of Nelson-Hall Pub-

Preface

lishers; Sheila Whalen our pleasant, skillful, and always efficient project editor; and John Litweiler, our thorough and skillful copy editor.

CHAPTER ONE

Introduction

P. Nelson Reid and Philip R. Popple

This book poses a direct question: What is the moral justification for the professional existence and activities of social work? It asks this question of a number of social work academics, all presumably well prepared by years of thought and writing in areas related to this problem. The contributors to this volume have not approached the question of moral justification in the same way, nor do they reach consensus about important issues of professional purpose. But the vigor with which each contributor attacks the problem, and the resourcefulness of the arguments brought to bear, suggest a profession that is intellectually engaged and aware of the continuing importance of the question.

Our more treatment-oriented colleagues have often observed that inordinate attention to one aspect of a person's life frequently represents an attempt to avoid dealing with another, less pleasant or manageable, aspect. Thus, a person who devotes seventy hours per week to a job is often manifesting a desire to avoid family problems rather than a great love of or dedication to a career. We suspect that social work, with its preoccupation with "science" and with developing empirically validated practice techniques, is exhibiting this syndrome. As Siporin has contended, social work is basically a *normative discipline*. This contention is based on two observations. First, social intervention has consequences for people: It alters the distribution of things that are valuable to society. Social work, specializing as it does in certain aspects of that intervention, must inevitably face the issue of the philosophical basis for this redistribution. Second, social work concerns itself with human behavior, individually or collectively, which is socially defined as good, obligatory, and normal; or bad, deviant, and offensive. Social work,

1

whether regarded as a norm enforcer or a norm changer, must deal with the essential morality of these norms.

Morality, in the complete sense, is more than the simple categorization of things as right and wrong. It has to do with how persons ought to behave *on principle,* because a moral principle is an objective rule which when properly applied distinguishes between right and wrong. Such rules may be applied to the behavior of individuals, whether client or professional, or to social processes and their associated outcomes. Social work is guided by such moral principles, but they are rarely clearly and completely explicated.

So, then, what is the moral model upon which social work is based? What is social work all about in the larger sense, and what principles does it use to justify its activities and its interventions? "Social work for what?" is the question. Are we developing ever more effective techniques to serve a purpose which is moral and good, or are we simply increasing the armamentarium of oppression, as the left would have it, or of anarchy, as the right suggests?

This book attempts to address some of the moral issues contained in the question, "Social work for what?" It presents a collection of essays around a common theme: The moral justification for the existence of the social work profession, and of the social interventions in which those in the profession engage. What vision of the good does social work hold, and how has this changed or been reinterpreted over the hundred or so years of the profession's life? It is easy to assert the evident goodness of helping people, and it is commonly assumed that the professionalization of social work furthers that good. Both individually and collectively we are inclined to see ourselves as good persons doing those things which seem right. But goodness of motivation is only one aspect of morality, an aspect that may be unrelated to outcome. There is the possibility that our judgments are self-serving rationales rather than products of rigorous analysis.

In the title of this work we use the term "moral purposes," and the authors of the essays frequently use the term "moral philosophy." These terms have a rather old-fashioned ring and, indeed, are considered by some to be outdated. They refer to what is now generally dealt with under the term "ethics," a term which we find problematical because it is used in such different ways. "Ethics," for example, may refer to a general pattern or way of life, as in Christian ethics or Buddhist ethics; or "ethics" may mean a set of rules of conduct, as in the NASW Code of Ethics. "Ethics" is also used in reference to inquiry about ways of life and the implications of one's behavior for others. This usage concerns questions of what we regard as good and bad, and how we differentiate the values of the human things we do and see in social life. In social work "ethics" has come to be associated mainly with rules of conduct, but in this volume our concern with "ethics" is closer to the third use of the term. To avoid confusion we have used the older "moral philosophy," which we believe is more precisely descriptive of the questions we pose.

Analysis of such questions is no light labor. Quite by accident on the very day of this writing, one of the editors was having lunch with a professor of philosophy who has taught for nearly thirty years in one of the better southern universities. Many matters were discussed, including this book, and the philosopher made a startling comment; he said he "doesn't believe in ethics." It was explained that this book was not precisely about ethics; nevertheless, it was surprising to hear a professor of philosophy, of all people, say that he found no merit in the concept and application of ethical reasoning. "Nope," he said, "it's all axe grinding, all just high-sounding rationale for personal preference." We will leave it to the reader to decide whether this book is merely an exercise in axe grinding or not. However, it is good to bear in mind that some axes are ground considerably more finely than others, and that we have asked each contributor to explicate his or her arguments as clearly as possible so that we might examine each structure they have rendered, as a whole and in its component parts.

Common Themes

Each contributor to this volume was given the general assignment to analyze a topic related to the moral philosophy of social work. Common *professional issues* emerged in the authors' responses to this general assignment. One of the questions posed to each contributor was "How do we understand the *social intentions* of social work, both currently and in its past, and how may the profession and its members justify itself and themselves, in terms of their contribution to the good of people and of society?" Asking a profession to define itself in terms of its philosophy, and specifically its moral purposes, may seem unreasonable. Professions, after all, have taken to justifying themselves in terms of the power and effectiveness of their interventions, their elaborate bases of knowledge, and their ability to marshal this knowledge for some predictable effect. The professional literature of most professions searches primarily for justification in such terms, and social work has frequently been criticized for its failure to develop an empirically testable and proven form of professional interventive technology.

But power and technology for what? A profession, no less than an individual, must seek to make sense of its life and its time, to connect itself to some larger rationale that has a purpose beyond mere self-interest. A profession, by definition, is a group of persons bound to some creed which commits its members to something beyond themselves. What we seek is a current definition, in moral terms, of that larger social purpose of our profession.

Each of our contributors has sought to define this purpose in a way that provides some bedrock for social work, bedrock upon which the specific aspects of practice methods and interventive means and outcomes can be founded. We have neither sought nor achieved consensus, but certain themes do pervade these essays. These themes represent the central moral issues with which the social work profession must grapple: (1) The issue of social control—collective social standards and expectations versus individualism; (2) distributive justice—equality in power and resources versus strict equity in social transaction and tradition in social roles; (3) the no-less-relevant issues of fee-for-service practice as a profit-making activity, largely provided to a middle-class clientele, versus public sector social work and the primacy of service to the poor.

The apparent *decline of the welfare state* over the past two decades represents another commonly noted element in the authors' responses. Social work has felt threatened in recent years, partly in terms of its professional territorial grip and partly in terms of its political identity. It has been particularly forceful in defense of itself and of the social service system in general, as conservative political movements in the United States have eroded some of the programs and much of the ideology of Depression-era and post-World War II welfare state development. Recent developments in Eastern Europe suggest the birth of a new era in which the desire for individualism and free markets may cause a decline in faith in the state and in collective solutions to social problems; such trends may further undermine widespread public support for welfare state ideology and the related systems of public services.

Professional organizations representing organized social work interests have reacted strongly to cuts in domestic welfare programs and have often joined the chorus of cultural criticism that accuses our society of being increasingly selfish and class-divided. In recent years the profession has sounded as if it had a special mission that, by implication, was not fully shared by more market-minded professionals in the human services. The moral tone of such commentary, which suggests that social work is one of the final protectors of the collective social trust, questions both the nature of the profession's social commit-ment and the permanence of that commitment's ties to a power-ful state.

The erosion of the traditional welfare state and the emer-gence of a post-New Deal political order, in which old alliances and social agendas seem less relevant, have had a number of consequences. Among them is the ongoing restructuring of human services in the United States, tending increasingly to-ward private delivery systems—with state or insurance subsid-ies—and away from old-fashioned public agency provision. This has led in turn to a strong resurgence of the clinical practice model in social work and private practice. Such developments seem to challenge the sense of identity and moral purpose that has informed social work for much of the century.

The transition, perhaps incomplete, *from nineteenth to twentieth century ideas about human nature and life,* repre-sents another theme in many chapters. Social work has its roots in the nineteenth-century charity organization movement in the United States and Britain, and its early life, both professional and intellectual, reflect nineteenth century ideas about human character and social responsibility. The Progressive movement and the reaction to the more strident advocates of Social Darwinism gave social work a decidedly more environmental view, diminishing the emphasis on the personal responsibility of those to be served (but not of those doing the serving). But the largely individual treatment model of service, which came to be known as casework, would not only survive but prevail.

The subsequent efforts to establish social work as a genuine profession—complete with professional organizations, professional schools for training, and models of practice derivative of medicine—pose a number of questions. Is the private-practice model of social work compatible with the social commitments of the profession? Does the rapid growth of public social services in the 1920s and 1930s threaten professional standards and the supremacy of graduate education? Is the profession's close association with the state an indication of social control, and does the very conventional nature of social work inhibit true embodiment of client interests? Does the choice of practice models derived from Freudian psychology represent the status striving of the profession, or does this choice represent sound scientific judgment about the needs of its clientele?

For years much of the debate on these and many other questions was carried by the functionalist/diagnostic division in social work, and the field enjoyed the intellectual fruits of allowing identifiable schools of thought to compete for the hearts and minds of social workers. Some years later the debate would be renewed in a less comprehensive form, especially in regard to the poor, and the ideological wave of the sixties would bring to social work concepts of empowerment and liberation applied not only to the poor, but to many many others as well. In the backwash of this ideology, traditional notions of social normalcy and proper social functioning sunk out of sight, and the idea of a social work which could recognize and treat deviance seemed hopelessly outdated. More recently the profession of social work has endured disruptive changes, many of them reflected in the character and structure of the social services themselves.

The Contributions

Stimulated by a Winston Fund supported symposium on the "Moral Purposes of Social Work" held in the spring of 1988 at North Carolina State University, each contribution to this book is a major original work by its author(s). Most of the papers are in some way dialectical, in that they conceptualize moral issues in social work as choices between contradictory ideas.

In the opening essay Frederic G. Reamer introduces a number of moral issues of contemporary concern to the profession of social work. The focus of his essay is on the motivation of individuals for entering social work and on the profession's conception of the public good. He looks at competing conceptions of social work as a calling or a career and expresses concern that the career aspects of the profession are eclipsing the historical sense of social work as a calling. He argues that while it is certainly acceptable for practitioners to be concerned with their own well-being, an enlightened view of the public good requires that we conceptualize social work as a calling.

In the second essay P. Nelson Reid presents a more conservative perspective. He observes that social workers work in organizations in which neither the interests of clients nor those of professional social work dominate. He argues that social work stems from the major American and Western value of utilitarianism, and that as a result social work "is not so much concerned with reducing dissatisfaction, or making people happy, as it is with rendering them useful." Reid argues that because social work reflects the values of the society in which it is practiced, the ". . . overarching moral question for social work . . . has been . . . the fundamental moral justice of the social order, which values economic utility and allocates on the basis of equity (as opposed to equality), and the consequent morality of the claims that society, in its collective institutions, places upon individuals."

From the vantage point of a career spanning more than fifty years, Alan Keith-Lucas presents a highly personal view of social work's moral dilemmas. He argues that social work has virtually deserted the poor in its quest for status and social acceptance. He proposes two models of practice to correct this

situation—co-planning to substitute for the currently dominant therapeutic approach, and development of something similar to the British model of community social work in which
people are considered constituents rather than clients. He concludes his essay with the rather startling recommendation that
either psychotherapists should stop calling themselves social
workers, or people working with the poor and vulnerable should
find a new name for themselves.

In another essay with a conservative slant, Siporin argues
that social workers should serve as moral agents of society. He
believes that the libertarian ethic has pervaded society and
social work in recent decades and has resulted in social work
drifting away from its social assignment—helping people with
moral conflicts and dilemmas. He states forcefully, "Social
workers need to know clearly that they are agents of the community, with contractual obligations to represent the poor and
disadvantaged, yet serving and mediating the interests of the
poor and non-poor, the conforming and the deviant." He out-
lines a number of tasks which the profession should undertake
to "enable social workers to renew their crucial moral mission
in helping people to lead good lives in a good society."

The historical treatment/social change bifurcation in social
work is the focus of the essay by James O. Billups. He observes,
as do several other authors, that the treatment side of the
bifurcation is becoming dominant, and he argues that this results in a weakened moral vision in the profession. He asserts
that the only way this can be reversed is for practitioners,
educators, and students to return to a broad-scale commitment
to social work's historically grounded concern for both sides of
the person-environment complex. Three emerging approaches
are discussed which Billups believes may result in a more balanced profession—generalist, feminist, and social development.

In the next essay Elizabeth D. Hutchinson looks at issues
surrounding the use of authority with involuntary clients, particularly competition among three values treasured by social
work—protection of the common good, individual liberty, and
duty to aid vulnerable persons. She thoroughly analyzes conflicts among these values and concludes, "Social work authority
is safe only in the hands of professionals who can wrestle consci-

entiously with the ambiguities of social life." She concludes by outlining several practice principles to aid with this struggle.

The dialectical essays are capped off by a paper in which Popple asks why the intellectual history of social work has been dominated by analysis of various dualisms, such as cause-function and treatment-reform. He argues that these reflect the fact that social work has a built-in dualism which probably defies reconciliation. This dualism is that social work, as a profession, serves the social function of managing dependency so society can function smoothly. People who choose social work, however, tend to be liberal, sometimes even radical, and to see changing society as their moral purpose. Thus, social work is a profession with a conservative social function but a liberal moral purpose, and so will always be characterized by a dynamic tension between the two.

The final two essays are more exemplars than dialectics. In the first Wilma Peebles-Wilkins and Beverly B. Koerin approach the question of the moral purposes of social work from a different perspective. They observe that "The history of women in social reform, social welfare, and women's rights activities is largely written as a history of upper- and middle-class white women in the nineteenth century." They begin to correct this by presenting a piece of original historical research in which they look at community care emanating from the moral and social views of the late nineteenth- and early twentieth-century black community. They argue that from such historical analysis we can learn important lessons regarding contemporary service delivery patterns which require the creative use of social support systems, mutual aid groups, and other informal networks.

In the final essay Maria O'Neil McMahon emphasizes the need for social workers to recall their purpose and to find creative ways to respond to their calling, which she argues is to serve the poor and oppressed. She provides examples to show how the curricula of schools of social work can reflect sensitivity to the needs of the poor through appropriate content and experiences for students. She describes two ongoing projects which illustrate how social work programs can join in efforts to make a difference in the lives of poor populations in poverty-stricken communities or regions.

Taken together, the nine essays in this volume do not constitute a complete or systematic coverage of the whole topic of the moral philosophy of social work, nor were they intended to. They do, however, offer fascinating and thought-provoking perspectives on a number of key moral dilemmas. They often provoke more questions than they answer. This is good. We hope that this work will inspire further explorations into this most important topic.

CHAPTER TWO

Social Work and the Public Good: Calling or Career?

Frederic G. Reamer

To contemporary professionals, the concept of "calling" barely seems germane. What John Calvin had in mind when he referred to the "secret" and "churchly" call of the clergy—among the first learned professions—now seems anachronistic, out of step with the pace of modern professions. The public hardly views members of professions such as law, business, dentistry, and engineering as respondents to a call "without selfish ambition or avarice or any other selfish desire in receiving a 'preferred office.' "[1] Granted, professions such as nursing and social work may be viewed somewhat less cynically because some vestige of selflessness accrues to them, but the main point holds. Today the term "profession" is linked to careers or occupations whose practitioners may lack any sense of duty or mission.

That this is so even in a profession such as social work, which has historically been regarded as a profession dedicated to doing good, is sobering. A significant portion of the profession's members have abandoned their zeal for justice and public welfare in exchange for the pursuit of occupational security, enhanced status and income, and related perquisites. Along with the surrounding culture, much of the profession has turned inward, reflecting the widespread embrace of individualism infecting the nation. As Max Siporin has noted in his blunt critique of contemporary social work, "there is a prevailing cult of individualism that gives primacy to self-determination and autonomy; to self-development, self-enhancement, and self-gratification; and to a materialist competitiveness in relation to others. . . . The prevailing view of the human being in social work, and in our modern culture, remains essentially a psychological one."[2]

The dilemma is complex. It is well known that the mission

of social work has changed dramatically in recent years. Clinical social work, in the form of psychotherapy with troubled individuals and families, is in a period of ascendancy. The traditional partnership between social work and public welfare is now tenuous. However, this noteworthy shift of focus does not by itself signify the loss of a sense of calling. There are large numbers of principled clinical social workers who care deeply about the well-being of their individual clients and who, through their exercise of therapeutic skill, enhance the commonweal.

What matters is motive. In increasing numbers, social work is attracting practitioners with limited commitment to the profession's traditional concern with social justice and public welfare. Although today's social workers may be ideologically supportive of the profession's traditional values[3], for many this commitment is not what draws them to social work. Instead, the attractions are often professional advancement and autonomy, status, and financial security.

Yet we must not be fooled into thinking that this is a peculiarly modern development. Indeed, a close look at the historical record reveals an uneven past that foreshadowed the current dilemma.

The Emerging Profession: Beginnings to the New Deal

Social work has always struggled with the nature of its mission. Every serious account of the evolution of social work acknowledges the persistent tension between "case" and "cause," between amelioration of individual suffering and social change that addresses the structural flaws in the culture that foster the varied ills that individuals experience.[4] The profession's early concern with individual charity has its roots in the Bible and religion. Acts of charity were meant to fulfill God's commandments as much as to be genuine acts of kindness. As James Leiby notes:

> It is not necessary to belabor the historical link between religious charity and social welfare, but it is important to be clear about the relationship among the divine commandment of love, the idea of personal and social responsibility, and

the basis of public or governmental provision of help. . . . In theory, the responsibility was not between persons or between persons and an organized community, but between creatures and their Creator. Although the occasion for charity might arise from a personal or social difficulty, the act was not *in theory* a way of problem solving but a form of worship, a service to God in the form of a service to the person in need. . . .[5]

The Elizabethan Poor Law of 1601—commonly regarded as a landmark statute that synthesized earlier welfare legislation—had its origin in a system of poor relief provided by parishes of the Church of England. However, by the late-nineteenth century there was mounting criticism of religious charity, as reflected in the introduction of the still-current secular phrase, "social welfare." Religious charity frequently came to be viewed as moralistic, paternalistic, and disorganized. Although traces of Biblical influence can be found in the profession even today, the turn of the century marked a perceptible shift toward the secularization of welfare. In England, France, and the United States, this ultimately took the form of liberalism, which, in contrast to competing doctrines of collectivism and socialism, embraced the notion of individual rights and what Sir Isaiah Berlin calls negative liberty, or freedom from governmental interference.[6] It was in the midst of this era, filled with laissez-faire ideology and Social Darwinism, that social work got its formal start. Thus, it is not surprising that the earliest chapters of the profession's history focused on improving the morals of paupers. Walter I. Trattner conveys this paternalistic mood in his review of the early charity organization societies:

> Friendly visiting, then, assumed the right and the duty of intervention in the lives of the poor by their social and economic betters. The poor were not inherently vicious or mean. Rather, they were wayward children who drifted astray or who were incapable of discerning their own self-interest. They required no resource so desperately, therefore, as the advice of an intelligent friend who would offer sympathy, tact, patience, cheer, and wise counsel. The visitor's job was to discern the moral lapse responsible for the problem and then supply the appropriate guidance—something, of course, they were certain they could do.[7]

The winds began to shift by the early years of the twentieth century. The events and activities associated with the Progressive and settlement house eras and the nation's severest depression helped turn social workers' attention toward the commonweal. They could not help but recognize the need to examine the structural defects that created vulnerability and dependency.

But the enlightenment was only partial. As Leiby has shown, even following the Great Depression,

> . . . poor relief was sometimes justified as a means to prevent the public nuisance of begging, and the vagrancy laws were a means to deal with the nuisance of tramps. Community officials might take action because as Christians they had a responsibility to help or because they were looking out in a prudent way for what they took to be the best interest of the community. The right of a needy person to help was not a consideration.[8]

With the onset of the New Deal, social workers as a group were not well prepared to mobilize on behalf of the nation and its communities. Professional training typically emphasized therapeutic technique, but clients needed advocates, service brokers, and welfare administration and planning. The profession was employed largely in private agencies and clinics, while the new welfare programs were located in public agencies.[9]

The Bifurcated Profession: The 1940s to the Present

The aftermath of the Great Depression signaled an important split in social work's orientation toward helping. A significant portion of the profession continued to concentrate on therapeutic work, with an emphasis on individual change. The hunches and hypotheses of Freud, Jung, Rank, and Adler combined to stimulate what Kathleen Woodroofe describes as the "psychiatric deluge" in social work.[10] By 1940 any departure from a Freudian view in social work "was looked upon by some with the same horror as a true Stalinist appraising a Trotskyite."[11] In contrast were the practitioners committed to advancing public welfare and other programs begun under the New Deal. Their work was conducted in public agencies charged primarily with serving the poor, disabled, and those otherwise in need. Most were decidedly uninterested in providing psychotherapy.

But following World War II, the clinicians gained control of the profession and held it until the turbulence of the 1960s. Then the factions faced off again, with critics charging that social work had abandoned its social action mission and was not sufficiently concerned about converting private troubles into public issues. The titles of prominent journal articles during this period are revealing: Herbert Bisno's "How Social Will Social Work Be?," Martin Rein's "Social Work in Search of a Radical Profession," and Neil Gilbert and Harry Specht's "Social Work—The Incomplete Profession."[12] Although social workers embraced the Great Society and War on Poverty programs and policies, for many the grasp slipped as the public's faith in the efficacy of these initiatives declined.

The 1980s were reminiscent of the post-war years of the 1940s and 1950s when the relative tranquility associated with peacetime and domestic calm turned the attention of both the nation and its professionals inward. Pursuit of individual well-being became more compelling than pursuit of the public good. This was reflected especially in social work training programs. During the 1980s curricular concentrations in community organizing and social policy were either abandoned or left to limp along with underenrollment. In contrast, electives in casework and psychotherapy were filled to the brim. Freud returned, although some argue that he had never really left—had, at most, taken a short nap.

The data are compelling. Between 1972 and 1982 there was an 18 percent decline in the number of National Association of Social Workers members employed in the public sector, in federal, state, and local human service agencies. In contrast, employment in private sectarian agencies and proprietary (for-profit) agencies—the vast majority of which provide casework and psychotherapy services—increased 132 percent and 264 percent, respectively.[13] Further, between 1975 and 1985 the number of clinical social workers in the U.S. increased from approximately 25,000 to 60,000 (an increase of 140 percent), placing social workers first in the list of professional groups providing mental health services—followed by psychiatrists, clinical psychologists, and marriage and family counselors.[14]

Granted, this shift may reflect in part the decline since the 1970s in government funding of social service programs and in the number of jobs available in the public sector. The migration to the private sector of veteran government workers thoroughly frustrated by bureaucratic life may also be a factor. One also cannot assume that social workers engaged in private practice or affiliated with private agencies have necessarily shed their altruistic concern for human welfare issues.[15] However, the data strongly suggest a mounting neglect of public issues in favor of psychotherapeutic and casework services that for many workers may be more rewarding, respectable, and lucrative.

The Development of Professional Ethics

Social work's recent preoccupation with individual welfare is also reflected in the evolution of its ethical traditions, which presumably constitute the foundation of the profession. Attention to moral issues during the earliest years of the profession's history focused neither on the broad moral duty of society to care for its disadvantaged citizens, nor on the ethical behavior expected of practicing social workers. Rather, in the early days of the twentieth century the emphasis was on the morality of the profession's original clients—paupers. The literature of that era is replete with references to the unfortunate poor whose character and moral fiber needed strengthening to enable them to stand, however unsteadily, on their own two feet.[16]

From the Pauper's Morality to the Practitioner's

During the first half-century of social work's existence, a handful of local and national groups of social workers formulated draft codes of ethics for the profession. However, it was not until 1947 that the American Association of Social Workers adopted a formal code. In 1955 the AASW and six other national social work organizations joined to form the National Association of Social Workers.[17] It took five more years for that organization to adopt the first truly national code.

The 1960 code, which remained in force until 1980 (with a 1967 amendment concerning nondiscrimination), clearly acknowledged social workers' responsibility to address public welfare issues, in addition to meeting the needs of individual clients. Most of the code's principles were aspirational in tone, presumably intended to inspire practitioners rather than to provide strict guidelines for behavior (e.g., "I regard as my primary obligation the welfare of the individual or group served, which includes action for improving social conditions"; "I give precedence to my professional responsibility over my personal interests"). Perhaps reflecting the political and social climate of 1960, the National Association of Social Workers' first code, when it was introduced, clearly set forth social workers' obligation to attend to broad issues of social welfare and the public's interest. However, by the mid-1970s there was sufficient concern about the usefulness of the prevailing code that NASW established a task force to consider revision. As Charles McCann and Jane Park Cutler concluded in their well-publicized critique of the code:

> The sources of dissatisfaction are widespread and have involved practitioners, clients, chapter committees, and, in particular, those persons directly engaged in the adjudication of complaints in which unethical behavior is charged. At a time of growing specialization and organizational differentiation, a variety of issues have surfaced centering on the nature of the code itself, its level of abstraction and ambiguity, its scope and usefulness, and its provision for the handling of ethical complaints.[18]

The new code, which took effect in 1980, was much more ambitious in both breadth and depth. The principles were reorganized into six sections, addressing the social worker's obligations pertaining to conduct and comportment as a professional, clients, colleagues, employers, employing organizations, the social work profession, and society at large. Consistent with the resurgence of interest in individual welfare since the 1960s, and the movement of social workers into the private (especially mental health) sector, the 1980 code was devoted largely to ethical issues that arise in individual relationships of practitioners with clients, colleagues, and employers. Although a portion of the code clearly asserts social workers' obligation to address public issues (related, for example, to discrimination, access to social services, cultural diversity, duties during public emergencies, and social change), this section is overshadowed by the space and degree of detail devoted to the duties social workers owe individual clients, colleagues, and employers. This emphasis no doubt also reflects NASW's appropriate interest in devising clearer guidelines for adjudicating ethical complaints filed against members. In fact, according to the chair of the Task Force on Ethics responsible for the new code, the group's principal objective was to "formulate and organize principles of ethical conduct which prescribed or prohibited particular behaviors of practitioners, which could serve as the basis for the evaluation and adjudication of grievances and complaints about unethical conduct."[19]

The Changing Nature of Ethics

Thus, the meaning of ethics in social work has shifted during the profession's history, from the early concern about the morality of paupers to an enforceable ethical standard for social workers themselves. Several orientations toward professional ethics have been evident over the years, with varying degrees of persistence. Although they are conceptually distinct, these orientations are not necessarily characteristic of individual practitioners or discrete eras.

The *paternalistic orientation*—most clearly evident during the late nineteenth and early twentieth centuries, when friendly visiting and charity organization societies proliferated—is based on an assumption that the profession's public mission is to enhance the rectitude of its clients, enabling them to lead virtuous, wholesome, and gainful lives, independent of support from public or private coffers. The principal aim is to help the hungry, homeless, jobless, and destitute (and in some instances, the Godless) to muster their internal resources to lead more productive lives. Those who have strayed from life's straight and narrow path are to be helped to return to it.

In sharp contrast, the *social justice orientation* holds that dependency is primarily a function of structural flaws in the cultural and economic life that surrounds the least advantaged. Poverty, unemployment, crime, and some forms of mental illness are by-products of a culture that has lost its moral sensibilities. Over time the defects of capitalism and unchecked racism and other forms of oppression have produced a scarred underclass. The casualties of this harsh reality must be addressed by fundamental social change that pursues such goals as affirmative action, equality of opportunity, distribution of wealth, and humane welfare benefits and services that are not punitive in nature. Regressive taxes, unrestrained free enterprise, and robber barons must be replaced by forms of care driven by fairness, decency, and compassion. The profession's involvement in the settlement house movement, the New Deal, the War on Poverty, and the Great Society era reflects these views.[20]

Features of both the paternalistic and social justice orientations are present in the *religious orientation* toward social work values and ethics. From this point of view, a central mission of the professional—rooted in social work's historical link with the church—is to translate his or her religious convictions into meaningful social service.[21] Charity, for example, may represent Christian love, between individuals and God and among neighbors. It is not necessarily grounded in paternalism, but may derive from a sense of religious obligation.

Most recently the emerging emphasis on ethical dilemmas that arise in casework with individuals, families, and groups reflects a *clinical orientation* toward the place of ethics in social work. This current phenomenon—especially evident since the late 1970s—is part of the contemporary wave of interest in professional ethics generally. Central to it are discussions about such issues as client confidentiality (e.g., the duty to protect third parties, release of information, client access to records), privileged communication, informed consent, paternalism, truth-telling, conflicts of interest, whistle-blowing, and compliance with laws, and agency rules and regulations. Especially characteristic of this orientation is an emphasis on ethical decision-making and the resolution of conflicts of professional obligation.[22] This emphasis on ethical dilemmas is grounded in part in the profession's enduring concern about the relationship between clients' and workers' values.

A significant portion of current interest in social work ethics represents what might be dubbed a *defensive orientation.* In contrast to the clinical orientation, whose emphasis is on enhancing the ethical practice of social work primarily for the benefit of clients, the defensive orientation, focuses on the protection of the practitioner. It is based on concerns about allegations of various forms of negligence and malpractice, and it is dominated by concern about liability issues and the ever-increasing risk of lawsuits.[23]

This collection of perspectives on the proper place of ethics and values in social work is tempered by an *amoralistic orientation*, whose principal feature is the absence of normative concepts. This view is characteristic of practitioners whose approach to professional work is essentially technical. For example, many practitioners who participated in the "psychiatric deluge" of the 1920s avoided the language of ethics, substituting psychodynamic argot that, they hoped, would clarify the mysteries of human behavior. Modern-day social workers whose strategies are determined largely by allegedly value-neutral considerations such as psychotherapeutic techniques and program evaluation, and cost-benefit analysis qualify as well. Whether these tools and techniques are in fact value-neutral is irrelevant. What matters is practitioners' belief that this is so.

Competing Interests and the Public Good

The range of ethical issues addressed in social work clearly reflects the diverse aims of the profession and the mixed motives of its practitioners. Comparable diversity exists in all professions, of course. Each faces its own version of competing interests among individual clients, the public at large, and professionals themselves. Clients' individual interests may clash with the public's, for example, when the attorney-client privilege silences a lawyer who has knowledge of his client's involvement in an unsolved, heinous crime. Similarly, a physician who extends her Medicaid patient's hospital stay, not for medical reasons but because the patient is homeless, is caught in the rub between the public's and the client's interests.

Social Workers' Dilemmas

Social workers' versions of these dilemmas take several forms. A common one includes instances when protection of an individual client's interests directly threatens third parties. A client who informs his social worker confidentially that he plans to violently injure his estranged spouse presents the practitioner with a choice between the profession's time-honored prescription concerning privacy and the protection of a member of the public. Recent court decisions reinforce prevailing opinion in the professions that in extreme instances, typically when there is a threat of violence, the public's interests must take precedence over the client's.[24]

More controversial, however, are instances when a client's actions are viewed as an *indirect* threat to the public, through injury to the client him- or herself. As in other professions, social workers disagree about the extent to which clients have a right to engage in self-destructive behavior, and about the extent to which such behavior injures the commonweal in addition to the client. For some, bag people who are permitted to roam the streets and alleys of our cities, subsisting on others' remnants, threaten not only their own fragile well-being but also the public's sense of decency and morality. From this perspective, a society that neglects its most vulnerable citizens, in the name of negative liberty or for more callous reasons, is a public without a conscience; the truly helpless among us need to be protected for their own good and to preserve the moral fabric of the community. Where the boundaries should be drawn, of course, is not clear. Questions about the legitimacy of the public's paternalism pertain not only to the homeless, but also to others whose actions seem self-destructive, such as alcoholics, drug abusers, women who remain with men who batter, and those who are suicidal.[25]

It is not always the client's interests that compete with the public's, however. Not infrequently, it is the interests of professionals that produce a clash. As noted above, in recent years there has been an increase in the number of social workers engaged in proprietary pursuits, in the form of private practice or through vested interests in profit-making ventures such as nursing homes, counseling and psychiatric treatment centers, and private-sector prisons. Participation in such profit-sensitive activities has created novel opportunities for conflicts of interest to emerge. Such professionals depend to a considerable extent on financial reimbursement by third-party payers (insurance companies and government agencies, in particular) whose disbursements ultimately affect the public's welfare, its pocketbook, and its access to social services at a fair and reasonable cost. Incentives abound for practitioners to manipulate lengths of stay, diagnosis, and treatment protocols to enhance reimbursement.[26] Professionals' motives in these instances are not always ignoble, of course. Such manipulation is often inspired by genuine concern for the client. Private psychotherapists who insert bogus diagnostic codes on insurance claim forms are not necessarily attempting to line their own pockets; frequently they are seeking a way to provide critically needed help to distressed clients who cannot afford to obtain services without subvention by a third party.

Professional self-interest is not always individually based. At times it is the profession *qua* profession that competes with the public good, by placing its own "corporate" interests above the public's—for example, by protecting itself from reasonable outside scrutiny or regulation, or by restricting access to the guild. It is typically claimed that admission to training programs is deliberately limited and that standards for licensure are artificially strict, so that competition is reduced and remuneration inflated. Such cynical and conspiratorial views, although frequently exaggerated, point to a serious credibility problem for the professions. Of course, they may also accurately reflect a genuine threat to the public welfare by virtue of a profession's greed.

While the problem may be less severe in social work than in professions in which there is greater demand for entry (and whose members enjoy higher levels of compensation), in no way is social work immune from the spirit of such criticism. Significant pressure exists throughout the United States to license and register social workers, establish certification examinations, and restrict the use of the title "social worker." Although such efforts are promoted in the name of quality assurance and public interest, mutterings about self-aggrandizing motives are growing louder.

Tensions *within* the professions complicate matters. It would be a mistake to characterize professions as monolithic entities whose members have uniform, homogeneous views of the public good. On the contrary, factions within professions lock horns on occasion by virtue of differences in their understanding of the public's best interests. Prosecuting and defense attorneys, for example, adopt radically different views of the interests that ought to be protected in a criminal trial. Although they may share a teleological belief that in the long run the public's interests are best protected by an adversarial system of justice, their views of their respective professional duties clash in the short run; one aims for conviction and public safety, while the other argues for acquittal and freedom. Likewise, a physician employed by a pharmaceutical house may argue before the U.S. Food and Drug Administration that an experimental drug is ready for commercial sale, while her medical counterpart employed by the FDA claims that marketing the drug would imperil the public's health. Similarly, a social worker functioning as a caseworker in a community mental health center may have a markedly different view of the need for increased welfare benefits than does the social worker who is a public administrator charged with fiscal responsibility for the state's welfare budget.

The Influence of Professional Goals

Thus, as with other professionals, social workers' conceptions and pursuits of the public good depend to a considerable extent on the nature of their professional goals, the means used to pursue them, and the organizational contexts in which they work. Patterns exist. For social workers who seek first and foremost to preserve social order, the public good may be enhanced through forms of social control, such as punitive and restrictive welfare regulations. Eligibility criteria for public aid benefits may be based primarily on judgments about what will best maintain the status quo. From this perspective, the preservation of social order takes precedence over individual clients' demands or interests when welfare recipients clamor for more generous benefits. Such social work functions are most likely to be performed in bureaucratically dominated public agencies, governed by formal regulations, centralized power, and formal hierarchies of authority that limit professionals' discretion.[27]

At the other extreme are radical social workers who challenge conventional policies, regulations, and assumptions related to social welfare. The public's interests may be promoted by use of controversial tactics designed to disrupt and undermine practices and policies that oppress the downtrodden. These professionals may organize rent strikes to provoke slumlords, boycotts to challenge unfair labor practices, and demonstrations to embarrass and pressure unresponsive public officials. They are likely to work out of inadequately funded, informally organized, democratically run agencies that claim to serve the people. In cases of conflict, the public good is served by razing bureaucratic, economic, and political barriers that interfere with meeting the needs of the masses.

Between these extremes are the social workers who are inclined to negotiate diplomatically about policies and programs in order to address clients' needs, and to advocate in a moderate rather than a radical or provocative fashion constructive social change. For this group, the public is best served by strategies such as education, lobbying, and traditional social services. Emphasis is on working with and within the system to prevent social problems, to respond to those in need or vulnerable, and to restore the disabled to some modicum of health. Such work tends to be carried out in settings such as family service agencies, community mental health centers, health care settings, public welfare agencies, private practices, programs for the aged, child welfare agencies, schools, and emergency shelters. Whose interests should take precedence when clients' interests clash with the public's is often not clear to these more moderate social workers.

What distinguishes these wide-ranging views of the public good is, in part, the degree of emphasis placed on *consensus* and *conflict* as means of promoting the public interest. For radical social workers, conflict with those who occupy seats of power is essential. Otherwise, social change will be slow or impossible. As Philip R. Popple notes, from the point of view of the conflict model, moderate social workers "primarily function as minions of the elite, helping to keep the masses in line so they do not challenge existing institutions."[28]

For different reasons, conflict is also favored at times by social workers whose responsibilities serve a social control function. Here, conflict with antagonists may be engaged in to preserve the status quo, not to alter it. Restrictive or punitive welfare programs and policies may be designed in part to discourage the use of public aid, to bolster employment, and ultimately to sustain the free enterprise and market economy upon which capitalism depends. Thus, some form of conflict may be an important ingredient in both the radical and social control camps of the profession.

In contrast, more moderate social workers may prefer a greater use of consensus to promote the public good. Cooperation, collaboration, and mutual assistance are valued as both means and ends. Prevailing programs and policies may not be adequate, given the compelling needs of private citizens, yet their revision need not depend upon warfare among competing interests. Rather, more civilized forms of problem-solving are called for, the goal of which is agreement about the most efficient and fair response to pressing needs. Compromise may be essential rather than abhorrent. The consensus model assumes that the interests of the individual and society coincide and, therefore, that social work should seek to promote the interests of all individuals and groups.[29]

Although there have been glimmerings of radical social work throughout the profession's history, social workers by and large have favored consensus over conflict. This is especially so in the current chapter of the profession's history, when the majority of social workers are engaged in some form of casework or clinical practice. Not surprisingly, the public issues social workers now champion have shifted as well. While substantial numbers of practitioners continue to advocate on behalf of the poor and disadvantaged[30]—for welfare benefits, employment, training programs, health care, affordable housing, and the like—the debates most likely to attract attention concern issues that bear on the practice of clinical social work—licensing and registration, mandatory insurance coverage of social work services, and third-party reimbursement. These are not unimportant issues, yet they have altered the nature of the profession's audible and visible involvement in public discourse about social problems. The significance of this shift in emphasis is especially striking because of the common use by social workers of the rhetoric of "the public's best interest" and "the public good" in their advocacy of measures that advance the interests of professionals themselves.

Toward an Enlightened View of the Public Good

It is clear that interpretation of "the public good" varies depending upon one's professional aims. Vested interests are important determinants of perspective. At times throughout the profession's history, social workers have assumed an *enlightened view* of the public good, characterized by advocacy whose primary focus was the interests of the general citizenry and of individual clients, especially the most vulnerable and least advantaged. Concern with professional self-interest is secondary, from this point of view. Social action and social services designed to meet the needs of the indigent, abused, neglected, mentally ill, disabled, infirm, and of disaster victims and others are central to the mission of the profession.

In contrast, a *narrow view* of the public good is characterized by activities that serve primarily to advance the interests of practitioners and other members of the elite, with only secondary concern about the consequences for the public. Efforts to license and register social workers, promote reimbursement by third parties, and market services to public and private agencies are paradigmatic examples, when they are motivated primarily by self-interest. Although in fact the public may benefit from such activities, in the form of enhanced quality control in the delivery of services, and while large numbers of professionals no doubt promote such measures sincerely and altruistically, a portion of the social work profession seems driven to a considerable extent by the benefits that are likely to accrue to practitioners themselves.

As social workers pursue private, proprietary, and autonomous practice with greater frequency, lobbying on behalf of such measures as licensure and reimbursement becomes more and more essential to solvency and profit. Unfortunately, such a trend is accompanied by significant financial (and perhaps status-sensitive) incentives to cater to more rather than less affluent clients, especially those covered by generous insurance benefits or able to pay for services out of pocket. Thus, rather than pursuing the public good in a truly enlightened fashion,

the public may be served by a significant number of practitioners who can, at best, be described as pursuing "enlightened
self-interest."

The distinction between the genuinely enlightened and the
narrow views of the public good is evident in other professions
as well. Examples of an enlightened view include physicians
who volunteer their time to promote public health issues or
provide free health care to indigent patients; attorneys who
offer *pro bono* legal services to civic groups or non-profit organizations; business people who sponsor job training programs for
the disabled with little or no concern about tax credits; and
journalists who engage in investigate reporting because of their
deep-seated concern about public corruption. Examples of a
narrow view of the public good include physicians who favor
restricting admission to medical schools in order to limit competition and enhance the income of medical professionals,
while arguing that such measures are necessary to preserve
quality health care; attorneys who favor unrestricted, multime-
dia advertising to enlarge their clientele, while arguing that
they are merely responding to the public's need to be informed
about legal services; business people who lobby for import quo-
tas to sustain demand for their domestic products, while arguing about the threat that foreign imports pose to the nation's
economy; and journalists who oppose any restrictions on the
publication of sensationalized information about controversial
public figures, while promoting the public's right to know and
the journalist's duty to inform.

A Return to the Calling

It may be that the current preoccupation with clinical issues
in social work does not portend a permanent decline in the
profession's commitment to an enlightened view of the public
good. Every profession experiences pendular shifts in ideology;
today's fashion may be tomorrow's memory. Nonetheless,
some changes in ideology are not temporary. Some represent
fundamental changes in a profession's orientation. Is social
work on the cusp of just such a change? Now that social workers
are the largest provider in the U.S. of mental health services,
will they seek to match the income and prestige ordinarily

associated with professions such as psychiatry and psychology? What lasting effects will such a trend have on the value base of the profession and the goals of practice? As Siporin observes in his perceptive essay on the evolution of social work:

> In the history of social work as a profession, social workers clearly and consistently had a public image and public position as moral agents of society. They were seen as such because of their role in helping people to find and choose ways of individual and social functioning that they themselves and the general society could consider "right" and "good." Social workers stood and fought for certain values, some of which were not generally accepted or implemented by the larger society. They took the traditional values of charity and justice, inspirited them, and gave them secular and expanded definitions. These were then used to establish a new set of moral and ethical principles as well as social institutional provisions for the "social welfare." Welfare, as Frankel said, is a "moral ideal." The welfare to be protected and enhanced was that of all the people in society—the poor, minorities, and the disadvantaged, as well as the rich and privileged. . . . In recent years, however, this social work value system and its moral vision have been fragmented and weakened.[31]

The profession's ability to inspire an enlightened view of the public good will depend to a considerable degree on the motives of those admitted to and comprising its ranks. The more social work mimics professions that serve more affluent, advantaged clients, the less likely it will be to attract people committed to traditional social work values. Regrettably, one of the ironies of the profession is that its ability to fulfill its traditional mission seems inversely related to the value of the perquisites earned by its members.

To reclaim its enlightened view of the public good, social work must once again resemble a (secular) calling. One serves—primarily because one cares deeply about matters of social justice—those who are disadvantaged and oppressed, and those who are at risk. Gratification is primarily derived from knowing that one has responded to one of life's principal duties to others.

This is not to suggest that a professional career demands an ascetic lifestyle and the complete forfeiture of status and comfort. The profession's ranks surely would be thin were such a standard in force. Moreover, there is no evidence to suggest that healthy employment dividends necessarily corrupt. The world is full of remarkably dedicated professionals who happen to be amply rewarded for their talents and efforts. Such rewards may even enhance their ability to contribute as much as they do.

Motive is key, however. In the final analysis a truly enlightened view of the professional's role in promoting the public good elevates mission above self-interest. A professional motivated exclusively or primarily by self-interest may ultimately produce the same good in the world as the altruist, if the measurement is lives saved, courtroom victories won, or psychoses cured. One would hardly consider the former's efforts enlightened, however. Gustafson states the case well for social workers:

> I suppose that studies have been made of the motives of persons going into the learned service professions; I have not attempted to search for such. My impression is that for many persons, especially those going into relatively low-salaried service professions, the incentive is a deeply moral one. The presence of poverty, social disorganization, disease, personal anguish, injustice in the distribution of human services , ignorance, and similar factors move persons to seek the education and training to relieve these impediments to human fulfillment. Incentive might well go beyond relief from suffering and avoidance of evil; persons see unfulfilled possibilities in the lives of individuals, groups, and communities which might be better realized by conscientious and competent professional activity. Such motives and incentives are not primarily self-interested; persons of great ability could certainly receive greater financial remuneration and status in other occupations. These moral motives are part of a "calling."[32]

An enlightened view of the public good—social service in response to a calling—entails some form of sacrifice. We attend to others because it matters to us that their needs be met somehow, preferably in a way that discourages dependency and paternalism. Self-interest is not our primary concern. Unfortunately, contemporary professionalization, bureaucratization, and institutionalization of social services lead to an emphasis on social work as a career or occupation, rather than as a genuine calling. As Gustafson queries:

> Has the development of institutionalized ways of meeting the needs of those who cannot afford services (done very properly, I want to stress, for the sake of distributive justice) altered the outlook and motivation of members of the professions? Does a profession which exists to meet human needs lose something of the sense of its intrinsic character as a profession when there are few occasions in which the exercise of the profession requires some self-denial on the part of the practitioner?[33]

Indiscriminate helping, of course, is naive and possibly harmful. Selfless social workers who function as loose cannons can be intrusive, coercive, arrogant, and patronizing. The undisciplined assistance such practitioners deliver, thinly disguised as altruism, can actually threaten the public good. As James F. Gustafson argues, "A calling without professionalization is bumbling, ineffective, and even dangerous. A profession without a calling, however, has no taps of moral and humane rootage to keep motivation alive, to keep human sensitivities and sensibilities alert, and to nourish a proper sense of self-fulfillment. Nor does a profession without a calling easily envision the larger ends and purposes of human good that our individual efforts can serve."[34]

It is not fair, of course, to place the burden entirely upon the shoulders of individual professionals. Both the public and private sectors must demonstrate an ideological commitment to welfare (in the grand sense of the term) and a willingness to allocate the financial resources required to care for those who are dependent. It would be presumptuous to exhort social workers to train for jobs that do not exist and for a mission that is not supported in earnest by the broader culture.

It is inevitable that professionals' perceptions of the public good will vary, and that impediments will interfere with efforts to promote it. Conflicts of interest between the public on one hand, and clients, professionals, and the professions themselves on the other, will persist. If professionals wish to claim that their raison d'etre is service to the public, they will need to persuade their audience that their intentions are indeed noble. In the case of social work, the challenge is especially substantial because of the tempting, previously untapped pathways to professional status and gain. Should the profession succeed in its efforts to sustain its traditional mission, it will have regained what Siporin describes as "its moral vision and idealism and even the moral passion that the old-time social workers had."[35] Should it fail, contemporary professionals will have lost an important lodestar in their efforts to clarify the essential bond between their work and the public good.

Notes

This work was supported in part by the Hastings Center and The Walter and Elise Haas Fund.

1. James F. Gustafson, "Professions as 'Callings,' " *Social Service Review* 56 (1982): 502–503.

2. Max Siporin, "Moral Philosophy in Social Work Today," *Social Service Review* 56 (1982): 527–28. Also see Siporin's discussion, in chapter 5 of this volume, of the impact of libertarian instincts on social work's mission.

3. In Linda Cherrey Reeser and Irwin Epstein, *Professionalization and Activism in Social Work* (New York: Columbia University Press, 1990).

4. See Popple, chapter 8 in this volume, for a detailed discussion of this point.

5. James Leiby, "Moral Foundations of Social Welfare and Social Work: A Historical Review," *Social Service Review* 30 (1985): 324.

6. Isaiah Berlin, *Four Essays on Liberty* (Oxford: Oxford University Press, 1968).

7. Walter I. Trattner, ed., *From Poor Law to Welfare State*, 2nd ed. (New York: The Free Press, 1979), 85.

8. Leiby, "Moral Foundations," 326.

9. Philip R. Popple, "The Social Work Profession: A Reconceptualization," *Social Work Review* 59 (1985): 565.

10. Kathleen Woodroofe, *From Charity to Social Work in England and the United States* (Toronto: University of Toronto Press, 1962), 118–47.

11. Arthur P. Miles, *American Social Work Theory* (New York: Harper & Row, 1954), 9. Cited in Woodroofe, *From Charity to Social Work*, 130.

12. Herbert Bisno, "How Social Will Social Work Be?" *Social Work* 1 (April 1956): 12–18. Neil Gilbert and Harry Specht, "Social Work—The Incomplete Profession," *Social Work* 19 (November 1974): 665–74. Martin Rein, "Social Work in Search of a Radical Profession," *Social Work* 15 (April 1970): 13–28.

13. "Membership Survey Shows Practice Shifts," *NASW News* 28 (1983): 6.

14. Daniel Goleman, "Social Workers Vault into a Leading Role in Psychotherapy," *New York Times*, 30 April 1985: C-1, C-9.

15. Reeser and Epstein, *Professionalization and Activism*.

16. Frederic G. Reamer, "Ethical Content in Social Work," *Social Casework* 61 (1980): 531–40.

17. Arlien Johnson, "Educating Professional Social Workers for Ethical Practice," *Social Service Review* 29 (1955): 125–36.

18. Charles W. McCann and Jane Park Cutler, "Ethics and the Alleged Unethical," *Social Work* 24 (1979): 5.

19. Charles Levy, "Conflicts and Considerations in the Process of Code Revision: The Challenge to the NASW Task Force on Ethics," (Unpublished manuscript).

20. Allen F. Davis, *Spearheads for Reform* (New York: Oxford University Press, 1967).

21. Robert T. Constable, "Values, Religion, and Social Work Practice," *Social Thought* 9 (1983) 4: 29–41. Martin E. Marty, "Social Service: Godly and Godless," *Social Service Review* 54 (1980): 463–81.

22. Frederic G. Reamer, "Values and Ethics," in *Encyclopedia of Social Work*, 18th ed. (Silver Spring, Md.: National Association of Social Workers, 1987), 801–809; idem, *Ethical Dilemmas in Social Service* (New York: Columbia University Press, 1990): 179–223.

23. Frederic G. Reamer, "Liability Issues in Social Work Supervision," *Social Work* 34 (September 1989): 445–48.

24. Marjorie B. Lewis, "Duty to Warn versus Duty to Maintain Confidentiality: Conflicting Demands on Mental Health Professionals," *Suffolk Law Review* 20 (1986): 579–615.

25. Frederic G. Reamer, "The Concept of Paternalism in Social Work," *Social Service Review* 57 (June 1983): 254–71; idem, "Toward Ethical Practice: The Relevance of Ethical Theory," *Social Thought* 15 (1989) 3: 67–78.

26. Stuart A. Kirt and Herb Kutchins, "Deliberate Misdiagnosis in Mental Health Practice," *Social Service Review* 62 (1988): 225–37. Herb Kutchins and Stuart A. Kirk, "The Business of Diagnosis:

DSM-III and Clinical Social Work," *Social Work* 33 (May, 1984) 8: 215–20.

27. Yeheskel Hasenfeld, *Human Service Organizations* (Englewood Cliffs, N.J.: Prentice-Hall, 1983, 12–49.

28. Popple, "The Social Work Profession," 572.

29. Ibid., 571–72.

30. Reeser and Epstein, *Professionalization and Activism*, 9–31.

31. Siporin, "Moral Philosophy," 518–19.

32. Gustafson, "Professions as 'Callings,' " 511. Also see Billups (chapter 6) and Keith-Lukas (chapter 4) in this volume for extensive discussions of challenges to social work's traditional mission.

33. Ibid., 509.

34. Ibid., 514.

35. Siporin, "Moral Philosophy," 530.

CHAPTER THREE

The Social Function and Social Morality of Social Work: A Utilitarian Perspective

P. Nelson Reid

Social work as an identifiable profession is only about a hundred years old. Emerging from the late-nineteenth century charity movement, and informed and invigorated in the U.S. by the subsequent Progressive reform movement of the early 1900s, it has developed all the trappings of full professionalism. That is, it is complete with systems of credentials, undergraduate and graduate professional training programs in universities and colleges, an international presence, and reasonably discrete arenas of practice dealing with all manner of human problems, misery, needs, and desires.

Before organized social work, there was the church, and for a time a "public" system of churchlike charitable aid. The profession of social work, emerging at the end of the public charity period and just prior to the twentieth century welfare state, benefited from the general decline of clerical power in the eighteenth and nineteenth centuries. It was part of the rise of a secular intellectual and professional order that would lay claim to the guidance of persons and society, guidance that had once been a clerical function. Many newer professions that emerged in the late 1900s, including social work, journalism, and economics, would be characterized as "preachers without pulpits" for the very good reason that they aspired to supply understanding and direction in the vacuum left by the church, and operated from inspiration as much as science. Social work, thus, has had a quite overt moral quality from the beginning.

Social work has been true to its origins over the years, in the sense that it has both carried on the intellectual tradition

that gave rise to the profession and maintained its strong element of moral judgment about society and persons. In its concern with those aspects of personal and community life that in
earlier times would be construed as having moral elements, in
its commitment to the basic technology of casework derived
from its charity organization days, and in its commitment to
social reform derived mostly from its link with Progressivism,
it reflects the influential ideas and movements in the society
from which it emerged. Indeed, social work's commitment to
the not-always-compatible ideas of casework and social reform
is what gives the profession its intriguing character, and continues to be the principal structure in the struggle for the souls of
the profession and its members.

This problem, of the dual individual/social reform character
in the profession, has made the search for a satisfying definition
of social work rather difficult, and has been puzzling to social
work practitioners and academics when they were asked the
inevitable question, "What do social workers do." The answers
may initially be constructed in terms of what specific tasks are
performed by a social worker or group of workers, and where,
or in what problem context, such work is carried out. But in the
end this sort of response is less than satisfying. The definition of
any profession is incomplete if it describes only the profession's
technical skills or the organizational context within which it
plies its trade; it must also include the matter of what social
purpose the profession performs, and to what good effect.

The search for the good purposes of social work and the
moral constructs that undergird those purposes must necessarily begin with a general definition of the social purposes of the
profession. But it cannot end there, so this chapter shall consider both the social function of the profession and what moral
justification such a function might have.

The Social Purpose of Social Work

Despite the many methods and fields of social work throughout
its history, it is possible to generalize that social work's principal claim to specialization has been what Charles Atherton,
Philip R. Popple, and others term the regulation of "dependence."[1] "Dependence" here means a state of non-production

in the social sense, of not having a self-sustaining social role that is regarded as having utility, not being sufficiently useful to others and to society. This implies something more than simple economic dependence, although that is a major category of dependence. The poor are certainly characterized by lack of income, but they have also been, both historically and currently, characterized as deficient in the performance of "legitimate" social roles in the family, the occupational order, and the community.

The problems of mental illness, child welfare, and chemical abuse, are likewise constructed in terms of normative social functioning, always implying some aspect of self-support and independence. Thus, the history of the social services in the United States has been one of tangible social benefits bound with efforts to rehabilitate and reform individual behavior. In every category of dependence there is a mixture of protection, compensation for the consequences of dependence, efforts to reform the dependent, and perhaps efforts to reform the social order so as to prevent dependence (sometimes by defining it away). As Joel F. Handler makes clear, this combination has given social work a special character, and requires of the worker a certain discretionary judgment.[2] Such discretion is the essence of professionalism, a professional being by definition one who is delegated social authority to make such judgments. The social work profession has specialized in the delivery of social services in a context that allows discretionary judgments in pursuing the reform of dependents. Dependence is the type of deviance around which social work has based its claim for professional authority and autonomy in child welfare, public assistance, mental health, medical social services, and elsewhere.

Dependence is a complex concept with various subtleties in different contexts. For example, children are by the nature of their social role allowably dependent, but such dependence must be managed so that progressive reduction of dependence on parents develops, and the child achieves a suitably self-sufficient social role. This process is extraordinarily important to society, which depends on the development of citizens who contribute to the interests of others through economic, familial, and community structures. If this important process is threatened, say by abuse or neglect, the state may assume some control of it. This responsibility is, of course, what child welfare is all about.

It is ironic that the main function and most challenging philosophic aspect of social work—the control of dependence— is so rarely considered in current social work literature. This apparent denial of the importance of dependence has much to do with developments in our culture which have altered or obliterated the definition of deviance, and have made it impossible to maintain professional judgment based upon normative concepts applicable to social behavior.

The idea of a profession having a social control function has not been well received in recent decades because the legitimacy of a society's interest in social control is no longer assumed. J. S. Lowell's late-nineteenth century observation about "the poor idlers, the failures, the broken-down men and women who could not stand the strain because of some weakness of mind or body or character" seems a bit harsh to our ears today.[3] Even Stuart A. Queen's much milder comments of the 1920s that social work will always exist to provide "service to persons seriously out of adjustment with their surroundings and to groups badly organized" implies some categorical judgement that would not fit well with social work today.[4]

The current lack of social consensus regarding the nature or existence of deviance—and the consequent problems of both classification and clarity of expectations—has created something of a problem for the profession. A major part of the problem is that the social service structure within which the profession is practiced has its roots in community expectations and collective responsibility and control. Thus, the social service structure reflects the notion of public or community provision of services to the needy (and presumably deviant) within the context of community expectations and collective values. That is, from the time these services were created, the organization of social services reflects their acceptance and understanding of the social control function. The result is tension between rules and regulations on one hand, and the interests of workers and clients on the other.

This long-standing tension, so well noted in Popple's contribution to this volume, has produced some interesting responses. One response is the romanticization of, and the flight into, private practice where the unalloyed interests of individuals—shorn of collective responsibilities to society, community, or even family—can be treated by social workers. These workers can presumably exercise their professional judgment in an optimum context, free of extraneous consideration and demand, accountable primarily to clients. An opposite response has been a popular embrace of a radical social criticism, which holds that social work, especially in its public service mode, merely represents dominant social class, race, or gender interests and, therefore, is inherently oppressive. The profession has been made to feel ashamed of its current and historic association with social standards, expectations, and control.

The modern view in social work, as Siporin has noted, is that "one should lead one's life according to personal choice rather than by the expectations of others." He observes that the profession has given itself over to a "prevailing cult of individualism which gives primacy to autonomy."[5] This emphasis on autonomy is partly derivative of the ideology of the field. For example, Piven and Cloward, widely read in social work education, have argued that the social control function has been the dominant function of most programs that have employed social workers. This function then, makes the

> disquiet (of social workers) understandable, for no professional wants to confront the possibility that the institutions with which he identifies and through which he finds his life work are fundamentally oppressive of the needs and rights of the dispossessed. Yet this is the lot of many of us in the field of social welfare, whether we are located in mental hospitals, the agencies of criminal justice and corrections, urban renewal authorities, or the income maintenance establishment.[6]

Characterization of the collective social values and standards of a community and society as "fundamentally oppressive" is the theme of these writers and many others. It is, of course, by no means self-evident that the interests of the individual clients of the "mental hospitals, agencies of criminal justice and corrections," etc., are to be regarded as morally superior to the collective interests of society, but much influential literature in social work seems to presume such community interests are oppressive and, therefore, morally inferior.

Irving Howe renders this same point about the oppressive social worker even more graphically:

> Beneath the lowest rung of society live the speechless. They are the broken and deranged, the flotsam and the *lumpen*, all those helpless people who have signed a separate peace with reality and now choose not to confront regulations, skills and responsibility. The hierarchy of class crushes them, but they do not form part of it. They are the waste of modern life, and they are kept going, and kept down, by agents of the state whom we call social workers.[7]

Howe wrote this in a review of Gyorgy Konrad's *The Caseworker*, a novel set in solidly statist Budapest in the 1960s. The hero, a child welfare worker, is:

> . . . a fairly decent and competent bureaucrat whose job it is to record the pleas, the lies, the revelations of his "clients" and then send them to some home, or to another office, or back to the street. A humane man, he is also a policeman regulating "the traffic of the suffering."

He wonders: "Who can cope with the battalions of misfits, the regiments of victims?"[8]

While this may seem a trifle dramatic, the essential issue is reflected in much social work literature over the century. Many social workers share both a sense of profound inadequacy in the face of "misfits and victims" and a feeling of being used to regulate suffering, while being given little role in shaping the terms of control. The history of social work thought is in good measure a history of the effort to make rational and just such a social function and occupational position. Konrad's caseworker certainly can't reconcile this apparent conflict between help and reform:

> My interrogations make me think of a surgeon who sews up
> his incision without removing the tumor. Something lies
> imbedded in the nature of things that is radically terrible, not
> so much evil in purpose or end as gratuitously malformed.[9]

What thoughtful social worker, or student, has not thought
such thoughts, and wondered, when all the therapeutic tinsel
and social service jargon are left behind, if the profession is
complicitous in some larger social engine that runs for no purpose in particular, and certainly for no *just* purpose.

But social control, if this means the integrating and com-
monality-building functions of a society, is not *inherently* oppressive. There is a distinction between oppression and rehabilitation, between intolerance and reasonable expectation. The
question is where the distinction is to be made; it will not do
to argue against the necessity to make the distinction.

Social work is certainly a profession tied to the most fundamental of society's functions, the control of those who are
identified as deviant. The poor, the insane, the criminal, the
dependent, the incapable—all those who for one reason or another do not share fully in the main currents of the society—
all are clients of social workers whose overriding function is to
render such persons into more nearly normative, contributing
members of the social order. The possibility of injustice in such
a function is clear enough.

But injustice surely does not always triumph. The educational system and the occupational order are powerful agents
of social control; both have potentially oppressive elements,
but the experience of most persons is not oppression. It is more
nearly a trade-off between freedom—of time, action, and sometimes thought and expression—and the real welfare benefits of
greater opportunity, social reward, income, and all that these
bring. Even the "total" institutions, represented by mental institutions and prisons, are not entirely exclusive of their in-
mates' interests. There is, even in these institutions, a process
of negotiation between the interests of the deviant and the
interests of the established. Eugene D. Genovese, the Marxist
historian, begins his well-regarded treatise on American slavery
with a quote from C. Vann Woodward:

The ironic thing about these two great hyphenate minorities, Southern-Americans and Afro-Americans, confronting each other on their native soil for three and one-half centuries, is the degree to which they have shaped each other's destiny, determined each other's isolation, shared and molded a common culture. It is in fact impossible to imagine the one without the other, and quite futile to try.[10]

Clearly, reciprocity is not necessarily justice, and does not imply an absence of oppression. But just as clearly, social control is not the one-dimensional process that the ideological use of the concept implies.[11]

This reciprocity, the elements of which change with time, allows both the maintenance of a stable social order and the management of social change. Social workers preside over one arena in which this process of change occurs. Whether it be public welfare, mental health, child welfare, corrections, family services, or virtually any social agency, social workers are involved not simply in oppression, but in managing, through a reciprocal process, what has been traditionally defined as "deviance." The function of the worker is, in a sense, to negotiate a settlement between the interests of clients and the demands of the dominant society, demands often expressed through organizational regulation or law. In virtually every social service there is an implied contract that involves an exchange of the service organization's resources for some behavioral concession on the part of the client. Sometimes such contracts seem hardly voluntary; they are enforced through coercion, as in the "suitable home" provisions in the earlier days of ADC. At other times the contract is based on less coercive elements, such as economic incentives. These contracts are implicitly short-term and subject to renegotiation; the contract between the state and the dependent, or the otherwise deviant, certainly changes with time—as is quite apparent in the history of social welfare.

The contractual element of social work practice is often very clear in the various methods of social casework, but the larger social contractual element in social services is often obscured. Konrad's caseworker, for example, seems to reflect the same sense of powerlessness and desperation he attributes to his clients:

> Go on, I say to my client. Out of habit, because I can guess what he's going to say, and doubt his truthfulness. He complains some more, justifies himself, puts the blame on others. From time to time he bursts into tears. Half of what he says is beside the point; he reels off platitudes, he unburdens himself. He thinks his situation is desperate; seems perfectly normal to me. He swears his cross is too heavy; seems quite bearable to me. He hints at suicide; I let it pass. He thinks I can save him; I can't tell him how wrong he is.[12]

The worker may be quite right that he cannot help and that some degree of pessimism is justified. But the basic system of many social institutions which exchange things valued for personal behavioral concessions need not be so depressing.

Many workers feel bound by "Rules and Regulations" (the title on Konrad's first chapter), yet these very constraints express the nature of the social work role. If "war is too important to be left to generals," as the old saying goes, then the public order seems to operate on the principle that "social control is too important to be left to social workers." That is true for precisely the reason that neither social workers nor generals are independent agents; they are carriers of collective will and purpose. So long as social work serves the poor and the deviant, the profession will continue to be constrained in service organizations in which the interests of neither clients nor professional social workers are primary.[13]

This of course raises the issue of social work as practiced privately, in non-public partnerships or in firms funded through client fees and insurance reimbursement. This may seem to suggest a social work absolutely free to pursue client interest, and motivated to satisfy that interest in order to increase income. But what one more typically finds is increased client choice and more decentralized provision of social work services, within the new constraints of public contracting, insurance regulations, DRG-type controls, and licensing requirements.

The development of a larger private practice field for social work is a major and largely positive development that has given rise to a more optimistic spirit in the profession. We have lost some of what Willard C. Richan and Allan R. Mendelsohn referred to in the 1970s as ". . . the indelible marks of an institution convinced of its own failure."[14] But this development is not entirely new. There have been previous tides of private practice, and there has been a long-term trend in social work to reduce its identification with the public social welfare system and the social services associated with social control. Instead, the profession has sought alliance with higher-status professions and has concentrated developing technically sound methods that apply to a broad base of clientele. The notion that social work has a principal moral, and actual, responsibility for the poor may have been well-accepted in professional circles in 1900, but as Frederic G. Reamer's paper in this volume argues, it is not evidently accepted among social workers today.

This is not to say that a broader outlook is undesirable or that attention to the technical aspects of social work practice is misplaced, or that private practice is a bad thing. On the contrary, each of these has been important in social work's recent development. But we must not lose sight of social work's historic relationship to the poor and displaced and the special place this gives the profession within society.

That place within the society is within what is usually referred to as "the social welfare institution." The social welfare institution, as it is usually described, concerns itself primarily with addressing the needs of the poor and potentially dependent.[15] Its purpose is to create for its clients and beneficiaries both a higher level of individual welfare and opportunity and an incentive to adopt the attributes of the dominant culture. Social welfare represents an attempt at constructing a contract between the actual or potential dependent and the larger society. The dependent, the poor, and the relatedly deviant are a significant problem to the social order, and to the state that is created to preserve that order. The nature of that problem is both symbolic and actual; that is, the poor represent the denial of the society's dominant images of justice, fairness, and payoff, and constitute a source of deviance ranging from "bad" language and behavior to political revolution. The control and reduction of such a population (consistent with the interests of the dominant portion of society) is obviously important business for most modern societies. It is precisely such a service that social welfare and social workers provide.

This most important social function is most clearly vested, ironically, in the very bureaucratic roles we professionals seek to be rid of. It is strange that, as a profession composed largely of persons who work in large and small bureaucracies, our images of ourselves, reflected in our educational literature and programs, seem more often based on a model of entrepreneurial practice in the classic professional tradition. Those images have never been reality for the great bulk of social workers; it would be better to embrace the reality that social work is not practiced *in* organizations so much as *through* organizations.

The Value Base of Social Work

The social function of social work is derived from society's need to regulate dependence, and that function is supported by culturally powerful systems of social thought and value. Consider the historical and current emphasis the profession places upon the notions of "rehabilitation" and "social functioning" as general goals of working with people. Despite the occasional suggestion that social work has a unique value system (which would be quite difficult for a profession considering the social requisites of professionalization, the central commitments of social work are derived from the central values of our culture. Social work came into being in the course of development of industrial societies. These societies, whether American or European, are based upon economic and political developments that involved the overthrow of privileged classes, and the rise to power of middle classes whose principal system of values was based on what Alvin Gouldner calls "utility."[16] That is, the middle classes were powerful because of economic developments that placed value on what they did.

The value of the middle classes was not a function of what they were, (as was the case with aristocratic classes) but rather of their usefulness. In the feudal order, the middle class had no place—not serf, not clergy, not noble—and ultimately came to pride itself upon its utility and to *measure the value of other elements of the social order by the same standard*. The middle classes mistrusted the aristocratic notion that the value of a man was a function of his birth. With the rise of the middle classes, we see the development of the political ideal of equality and the belief that the circumstances of one's birth do not determine the potential of one's life. This is why our political order is so evidently concerned with scanning for the useless and the parasitic. To some, the poor are suspect, others condemn the church or the corporation; but the basic value is the same: one has moral worth only to the extent that one is identifiably useful to others and contributes to the public welfare of society.

The idea of rehabilitation, so basic to the helping professions, rests on the dual foundation of utilitarianism—the idea that one should be useful, and liberal optimism—the notion that a free person may develop any potential. Without such faith in the potential to learn new behavior (as opposed to the belief that deviance is inborn and unchangeable), there would be no commitment to create utility, and the rationale of rehabilitation would never have developed. Nowhere has the value of utility been stronger than in the United States, and nowhere has the idea that the poor and the insane and the criminal are reformable been more influential.[17] Within this system of social value, social work was created, first stressing moral reform, later stressing political reform or liberation from unconscious motivation, but always emphasizing that people can be reformed and made more useful to their society. These value orientations certainly cannot be considered unique to social work. It is not without irony that the values that once fueled Western revolutions against class privilege and deterministic pessimism now seem to some regressive, but these values are nevertheless a major part of the philosophical heritage of the profession.

Social work is principally a response to utilitarian culture. The welfare state, particularly as it exists in the United States, and especially that sector of it staffed by social workers, is concerned not so much with reducing dissatisfaction or making people happy, as with rendering them useful. The continuing pressures to put welfare mothers to work and to find older people useful places in society attests to the strength of this passion. We live in a social order dominated by what Jane Adams long ago called "industrial values." Persons who expect to be valued must take their place in society and must demonstrate moral worth, not an inherent worth, but one earned in their own time.

Taken to excess, this idea of moral worth is distressingly demanding, unforgiving, and exclusive of human virtues that have no economic value. But in its basic elements such a value construct is a logical necessity for a modern society and economy, as Eastern Europe now seems to be discovering. And it is probably operationally fairer than other systems of valuation that must, of necessity, emphasize other characteristics such as political power, social status, beauty, parentage, intelligence, or ethnicity. Because of its impartiality it is the value system which is most likely to create an open system of opportunity for persons and to reward such persons for behavior contributing to the good of others. But it is not a value system particularly tolerant of deviation from the norm of usefulness, and it both assumes and sustains inequality even as it seeks to drive out inequity. For all of these reasons it cannot be said to be particularly kind to the incapable.

The power of this value system is amply evident in our social policy history. Take, for example, the distinction between social insurance and public assistance that is so basic to our income-maintenance system. As every student of social work knows, social insurances are well-funded, politically popular, non-stigmatizing, and relatively generous. The public assistance programs, on the other hand, are not only means-tested, but just plain mean: Low in benefit; high in stigma, intrusion, hassle, and political troubles; and susceptible to dramatic changes in law and regulation that reflect persistent displeasure with their operations.

The differences between public assistance and social insurance programs are so great, and the apparent advantages of social insurance so evident, that at least until the 1980s we pursued a policy in the United States of trying to make public assistance into social insurance or something rather like it. But there the worthiness problem thwarted us. It is the fundamental philosophical difficulty facing any social benefit program: Why should people be able to claim a social resource provided by others? On what basis are they worthy? Social insurances solve this problem by tying a contributory element to work. Future beneficiaries contribute to a trust fund and over time earn the right to the benefit. In essence the individual proves her or his worthiness by work and contribution prior to receiving the social benefit. Worthiness is then assumed at the point of eligibility.

Need alone is not sufficient to establish worthiness, however, so the history of public aid is a history of efforts to establish worthiness *during* the recipiency period. In the not-too-distant past this took the form of Suitable Home or Substitute Father provisions which sought to insure the exchange of benefits for right living. More recently the test of worthiness has become some variant of workfare and pursuit of child support. What the future may bring is not altogether clear, but the worthiness problem will not go away, because it expresses the most central of our cultural commitments.

So this is what social work is all about. It is a profession which, with some reluctance, accepts and administers the dominant utilitarian value system in our society while it seeks to rehabilitate the fallen and prevent dependence. This is social work's claim to social authority, its specialty, and social work carries it out through processes which seek a separate peace, a contract in which things of social value are exchanged for normative behavioral concessions from clients. But is this fair and reasonable? If this is social work's social function, can it be said to have a sustainable moral base?

The Moral Purposes of Social Work

Before Adam Smith wrote *The Wealth of Nations*, he had published a widely read *Theory of Moral Sentiments* in which he wrote:

> To feel much for others and little for ourselves . . . to restrain our selfish and to indulge our benevolent affections, constitutes the perfection of human nature; and can alone produce among mankind that harmony of sentiments and passions in which consists their whole grace and propriety.[18]

This may seem a very un-Adam Smith-like idea, but it reminds us that the ideas of free markets and free persons had a moral philosophical foundation. To Smith the problem was how to organize society in such a way as to make it more likely that persons would care for others. In *Moral Sentiments* he tells of a proper citizen of Edinborough reading in the newspaper of a horrible flood in China. The man is well-educated, religious, and quite moral, and he thinks to himself how very terrible the flood must be for the people involved. But he feels very little; thus, Smith recognizes the inherent limitations of human connection and care. He wonders, could there be some social arrangement in which the Edinborough gentleman's personal interests might somehow be served by his identification with the personal interests of someone in China? Smith found the answer to this problem in the market, in which persons, in pursuit of their self-interest, must understand the interests of others and seek to serve those interests well enough to be paid for it.

This in simple form is the basis of the notion that one's moral worth is tied to one's economic worth and that the duty to serve, "to feel much for others," is enforced through a market society. In this important sense the work of those in social work—to aid in the rehabilitation of persons, to allow independence, and to support a person's utility within the social order—is profoundly moral in nature.

Accepting these duties as moral does not solve all the moral problems in social work. There are still questions of distribution and the settlement of conflicting claims, for example.[19]

But the overarching moral question for social work in this century, posed time and time again in different forms, has been the question of the fundamental moral justice of the social order, which values economic utility and allocates on the basis of equity, and the consequent morality of the claims that society, in its collective institutions, places upon individuals. In order to pursue the moral nature of social work, it is necessary to consider the social function of the profession and the moral assumptions upon which such a function is founded. Such a consideration gives a direction which is quite different from that found within the bulk of social work literature. But it is a direction that *links* the profession, rather than alienating it, from the most elemental of our cultural ideas and forces. This different perspective places the consideration of questions about the place of the poor and dependent in the priorities of social work, as well as questions about public and private practice, in new light.

Notes

1. Charles Atherton, "The Social Assignment of Social Work," *Social Service Review* 43 (1969): 421–9. Philip R. Popple, "The Social Work Profession: A Reconceptualization," *Social Service Review* 59 (1985): 560–74.

2. Joel F. Handler, *The Coercive Social Worker: British Lessons for American Social Services* (Chicago: Rand McNally, 1973), 135–57.

3. William Rhinelander Stewart, *The Philanthropic Work of J. S. Lowell* (New York: Macmillan, 1911), 191.

4. Stuart A. Queen, *Social Work in the Light of History* (Philadelphia, Pa: Lippincott, 1922), 29.

5. Max Siporin, "Moral Philosophy in Social Work Today," *Social Service Review* 56 (1982): 519, 527.

6. Frances Fox Piven and Richard A. Cloward, "Reaffirming the Regulation of the Poor," *Social Service Review* 48 (1974): 1.

7. Irving Howe, review of Gyorgy Konrad, *The Caseworker*, in *New York Times Review of Books* (27 January 1974): 1.

8. Ibid., 28.

9. Gyorgy Konrad, *The Caseworker* (New York: Harcourt Brace Jovanovich, 1974), 63.

10. Eugene D. Genovese, *Roll, Jordan, Roll: The World the Slaves Made* (New York: Pantheon, 1974), Preface.

11. For a rather complete discussion of the nature of reciprocity in relationships between persons of differential power, see Richard M. Emerson, "Power Dependence Relations," *American Sociological Review* 27 (1962): 31–41.

12. Konrad, *The Caseworker*, 3.

13. If professional social work expands its service systems to include large numbers of middle class persons, the organizational character of the social services is likely to change. Middle class persons imbued with dominant social values and in a position to influence them are not likely to be subjected to service systems with the dual functions of personal service and personal reform. That is why services to the middle classes are characterized by private market delivery, or

some facsimile, while services to the poor typically have a non-market public service character, with consequent low-level accountability to its primary consumers.

14. Willard C. Richan and Allan R. Mendelsohn, *Social Work: The Unloved Profession* (New York: New Viewpoints, 1973), 73.

15. Harold Wilensky and Charles Lebeaux, *Industrial Society and Social Welfare*, rev. ed. (New York: The Free Press, 1965).

16. Alvin Gouldner, *The Coming Crisis of Western Sociology* (Garden City, N.J.: Doubleday, 1972).

17. David J. Rothman, *The Discovery of the Asylum: Social Order and Disorder in the New Republic* (Boston: Little, Brown, 1971).

18. Quoted in Gertrude Himmelfarb, *The Idea of Poverty: England in the Early Industrial Age* (New York: Knopf, 1984), 47.

19. P. Nelson Reid and James O. Billups, "Distributional Ethics in Social Work Education and Practice," *Journal of Social Work Education* 22 (Winter 1986): 1.

CHAPTER FOUR

A Socially Sanctioned Profession?

Alan Keith-Lucas

In March 1957, *Harper's Magazine* published an article by Marion K. Sanders, entitled "Social Work: A Profession Chasing Its Tail." The article is somewhat snide, but it rang a bell in the minds of some of us who had been social workers in the Depression of the 1930s. The blurb at the top of the first column read, "These earnest Do-gooders are so eager for dignity and status that they have forgotten what their job is . . ." The article complains that schools of social work "designed to furnish private philanthropic agencies with skilled social therapists" had "failed to produce either the leaders or the work force required by the changed and vastly expanded welfare born of the Depression and the Social Security Act of 1935." The social worker whose probably imaginary career the article follows leaves a big job in the public sector to become first a psychiatric social worker, then enters private practice in order not to lose her "professional skills." A board member questions the wisdom of "giving more and more intensive service to fewer and fewer people." Social work, the article says, "may have gained a profession by forfeiting a mission."

That article, I would contend, might have been written in even stronger terms today. Social work today has virtually deserted the poor. Most students applying to schools of social work do not want to be social workers. They do not want to dirty their hands with such mundane things as money, shelter, and clothing. They want to be therapists. Private practice is on the increase. As early as fifteen years or so ago a clinical social worker could write of private practice as enabling the social worker to exercise her skills "without interference from other priorities" and of "the necessity for social work to establish its identity as a profession, not a philanthropy."[1]

Those of us who were students or young workers in the 1930s were philanthropists in the original meaning of the word—those who love people—and did believe that we had a mission or, in Reamer's terms, a "calling," although we resisted the implication that its origin was religious. Religion, in the first flush of humanism, was identified largely in our minds with the more moralistic and evangelical Protestant sects. Catholics—such as Felix Biestek and Swithun Bowers, who appeared on the scene a little later—were allowed the language of religion to express their philosophy, but were seen largely as humanists at heart. Jews were respected for their commitment to social justice, but did not say much about religion. Nevertheless the new, more loving and affirming relationship we sought to cultivate with the poor and the oppressed was what we thought religion should be about, but frequently was not.

Our mission was to liberate people, from moralism, paternalism unjust laws, society's judgments, and the brutality of the capitalist system, just as Freud's—the early Freud, who was all we were officially permitted to know—was to liberate the id from the repression of the superego, which was one of the reasons we found his theories so attractive. Even Freud's determinism, as Lionel Trilling pointed out, was a liberating idea, for it freed humanity from being entirely at the mercy of the culture,[2] and Bertha Reynolds could say that it was no longer wrong to try to make people think and act as we wanted them to. In the long run it was simply silly.[3] In our view, it was also wrong.

Putting aside for a moment the niceties of Freudian and Rankian theory, what the psychoanalysts taught us was a new relationship with people. They stressed a sense of common human vulnerability, which was much enhanced by the Depression. Any of us might well be a social worker today and a client tomorrow. Indeed, in New York one had to be on relief to hold a social work job in the public sector. We rejected the role of managing or rehabilitating social deviants, which P. Nelson Reid seems to consider social work's main task. Our clients, most of them, weren't deviants, but our friends and neighbors, suffering, as we were from a mismanaged economy. Psychoanalysis also taught a view of a person not from the outside in, measured against some social norm, but from the inside out, from his or her own point of view; Martin Buber called this an I-Thou, not an I-It, relationship. And psychoanalysis stressed the enormous importance of human relationships.

True, we were mostly caseworkers. While we revered Jane Addams, the Abbott sisters, and Sophronisba Breckenridge, it was to the exponents of the new psychoanalytic theories that we looked for leadership—to Bertha Reynolds, Virginia Robinson, Jessie Taft, Florence Hollis, and Gordon Hamilton. The age of reform was over. We knew we did not have the clout of Jane Addams, for instance, who was one of several highly esteemed "good women, educated women and patrician women"[4] and the lifelong friend of senators and governors. We left reform largely to those who did have that clout—Harry Hopkins, Frances Perkins, Julia Lathrop, Fiorello LaGuardia, Senators Robert Wagner and Paul Douglas, many of whom had been Addams' associates. Most of us, too, saw what was happening in Washington—the Social Security Act, the National Labor Relations Act—as such an improvement on the past that there was not much to be done on a national level, although social work's more radical wing, social workers such as Mary Van Kleech, Frank Bancroft, and Irwin Epstein, were bitterly critical of the New Deal, both for what it did not do—Miss Perkins had given in to the American Medical Association on the matter of health insurance—and because of a deep suspicion of government as a whole.

But the dichotomy between the social activist and the caseworker was not so absolute as it might appear. Both were concerned with the betterment of society, but by different methods—one, as it were, from the top down, the other from the bottom up; one by changing the structures of society, the other by freeing the neglected or oppressed to take their rightful place in that society, and in doing so, reform it. There was to be a new, more egalitarian and participatory democracy, and social casework was to help bring it about. Writers such as Bertha Reynolds rejoiced in the new knowledge, not because it enhanced the professional status of social work, but because it freed people to be themselves. Even emerging technicians such as Gordon Hamilton insisted that their methods enhanced democracy and could exist only in a free society. Casework was idealistic. "At its best," said a writer some years later, "social casework can make the tenets of democratic living a deeply personal experience."[5]

Most social workers at that time saw themselves not as an arm of the culture or the society, but as an opponent of it, in both professional and private life. Bertha Reynolds worked for Harry Bridges' National Maritime Union, an avowedly Communist organization. The best social work paper of that time, *Social Work Today*, was, in the 1950s, placed on the Attorney General's list of subversive publications. Although it owed its existence largely to the rank-and-file movement of untrained welfare workers, among its contributors were many leaders in the field, including Grace Coyle, Karl de Schweinitz, Kenneth Pary, Katherine Lenroot, Frank Bruno, and more significantly, casework specialists such as Gordon Hamilton, Florence Sytz, Ruth Smalley, and Helen Harris.[6]

Social work also saw itself as aligned not so much with the learned professions as with labor. We joined one of the professional organizations, AASW, AAMSW, AASSW, or the like, but we were more interested in being part of the Social Service Employees' Union. John L. Lewis wrote an article in *Social Work Today* under the title of "Welcome Aboard, Social Work." The major policy course we were taught at school was "Labor Relations." We were, it is true, blind to the needs of minorities, which we saw as a lesser problem than the rights of the working man and the immigrant—our other "policy course" was "Cultural Backgrounds," largely those of Eastern Europe—but as a profession we were much concerned with our vision of the public good.

What happened to change our orientation and our vision of the good society? Because change it certainly did—and quickly. There are a number of explanations. Two sociological ones are the impact of the war, which put social reform on the back burner for a time and cost us our alliance with labor which was no longer a group struggling for its rights, but a full participant in a great national struggle; and the impact of the affluent society that succeeded the War, which dissolved our feeling of common human vulnerability. Those who were poor or unpopular in the 1950s were no longer people just like us; they were progenitors of an underclass whose rights became less important than society's need to alter their behavior. Social workers tend to reflect political trends as well, and the country was in a conservative, "don't rock the boat" mood.

But the philosophy of the profession was also changing. We were both Humanists and Utopians, but for the most part we had not, in the 1930's, become Positivists as well, and had not fully adopted the world view that I have elsewhere named Humanist-Positivist-Utopian—the dominant philosophy in America today. Positivism, the belief that Cartesian science can explain everything in this world, and that for something to be thought true it must be demonstrable by the scientific method, had been claimed by social workers since the days of Thomas Chalmers in the early 1800s. Those workers thought Martin Malthus's theories of population were "irrefragable as the most rigid demonstration,"[7] and could not understand why the poor wouldn't be sensible and stop having so many children. The Charity Organization Society had proclaimed a "science of social therapeutics"[8] and that "the principles of Organized Charity are the truth."[9] Jane Addams' work had owed a lot to its scientific tenor, although she refused to apply what she called a "pseudo-scientific" spirit to affairs of human conduct.[10] Mary Richmond's *Social Diagnosis* certainly looks to be scientific, although when she urged the establishment of schools of social work it was not so that students would know more, but so that they would learn "better habits of thought and higher ideals."[11]

And now there was Freud with an apparently new science, psychoanalysis. Despite the fact that Freud was actually as poor a scientist as he was a great philosopher—he extrapolated wildly from the particular to the general, and is even accused of having falsified some of his data[12]—it was as a scientist and not as a philosopher that he was acclaimed. Indeed, it is extraordinary what science was held to have accomplished, even justifying Freud's use of an "inside-out" (analytic) method rather than an "external" view, which is much more scientific,[13] and which is credited with discovering that starvation, punishment, and embarrassment are not effective social stimuli.[14] In 1941 Gordon Hamilton, in her somewhat intemperate attack on the Functional School of social work, said that we "could only have schools of thought until conclusive scientific data are secured."[15]

Social workers, of course, do need knowledge, and scientific research is one way of acquiring it, although one writer in the 1960s quotes psychiatrist Erik Erikson as holding that a strictly objective view of reality "represents the Cartesian strait-jacket that we have imposed on our model of man."[16] But an over-emphasis on science raises a number of temptations for a young profession seeking to help others. Science cannot deal with values, since values are not measurable. It has to consider values as either personal preferences or socially accepted norms. Indeed, Hamilton helped the profession identify itself with the predominant culture, when she quoted anthropologist Ruth Benedict to the effect that those whose "congenial responses" were in tune with the culture prospered and those who were at odds with it were "disoriented,"[17] thus giving rise to the concept of a "social norm" with which social work was to identify. This hardly leads to social reform, except in a society of contented cows.

Then again, a too-exclusive reliance on science tends to produce a very low estimate of the worth of one's fellows. Not only does it exclude many qualities of the more existential sort, such as courage, dedication, and the capacity for those ultimate emotions, love and joy, but it also focuses on what is wrong with those qualities rather than what is right. Jane Addams had seen that in 1899. A writer in the 1950s exemplifies this point. "Sharper social study methods," she writes, "and increased psychiatric knowledge bring us daily more usable information about the uncontrolled impulsivity, the impairment in capacity to form relationships and the ego and superego defectiveness of those whose social and emotional dysfunctioning comes to our attention"[18]—although this statement appears in an article urging greater accessibility of services. This kind of knowledge is a great temptation to pride. It shows little or no empathy, and it is hard to believe that the writer is concerned for the rights of people of whom she has so low an opinion.

Pride is, in fact, at the root of the problem. The medieval church recognized Pride, *Superbia*—a better term is perhaps "Arrogance"—as the Mother of all the Deadly Sins. The Greeks called it *hubris*. Theologically it means not only doing without God, but assuming God's prerogatives of omnipotence and judgment. In social work it is exhibited in pride in one's own knowledge, in claiming authority over others through that knowledge, and in being esteemed for this. The early Freudian social workers stood in awe of the new knowledge that they believed psychoanalytic theory offered. Bertha Reynolds cautioned workers to apply the new science "with all humility but with all the ruthless respect for facts which science demands."[19]

But humility is not a characteristic trait of the social scientist, or indeed of the humanist. Once he begins to think that he knows, he begins to claim a rightful authority over other people. In the 1940s a writer warned caseworkers in public assistance not to take unconscious advantage of their clients by virtue of their perceived authority to give or to deny a grant.[20] By 1954 casework was being described as "a highly skilled form of the exercise of influence,"[21] and four years later an article appeared in *Social Casework* under the title "The Social Control Function in Casework."[22] Social workers were also claimed to be "responsible" for their clients, even those who did not seek social work help, the "ethic of responsibility" being "set within a framework of knowledge and skills unknown to those who worked many years before us."[23]

In public assistance AFDC, which had been conceived and welcomed by social workers as a long-time rights program, providing money which could not be conditioned in any way, was fast becoming a program in which one was urged to become self-dependent as soon as possible, in which mothers were required to work outside the home, and in which the social worker had to devise a case-plan to get mothers off it as soon as possible. The watchword was "rehabilitation." Here was a vast reservoir of people who needed to be rehabilitated—not by empowering them financially, giving them something to depend on which Delafield Smith (a lawyer, not a social worker) had called a prerequisite for independence and the test of a free society[24]—but by virtual insistence on their use of a host of social services "more important" than financial aid. There were exceptions. One department in a populist state (Louisiana) held that its primary service was to procure for its clients the maximum grant permitted by law, and Alvin Schorr wrote "The Tendency to R_x."[25] But many social workers, paying lip service to the principle of client self-determination, still contributed to the erosion view of the program as a right. Gordon Hamilton said that "we do not have the common sense to insist on rehabil-itation in some categories of assistance," and, she added "insur-ance."[26] Another writer called children on AFDC "wards of the community," social workers, presumably, their guardians.[27] And Kermit Wiltse welcomed the reintroduction of Suitable Home provisions in ADC—a system in which social workers who disapproved of the conditions in a home could deny the family assistance, which was later declared unconstitutional—as "putting casework back into" the program.[28]

At the same time social work declared itself a "socially sanctioned profession." Who sanctioned it we do not know. Werner Boehm, in an article published in 1964, takes this social sanction for granted,[29] and in certain circles—the Army, for instance—he was right. In 1943 the Army did not even recog-nize social work as a civilian operation—the nearest they came to it was "personnel manager"—but by 1950 a social worker with a master's degree and ten years of experience could be commissioned as a lieutenant colonel.

What being a socially sanctioned profession and becoming more prescriptive has to do with working for the public good may not at first be obvious. Undoubtedly many social workers at the time thought they were serving society in a meaningful way. They were rehabilitating people. They were, along with other professions, such as psychiatrists, clinical psychologists, and various forms of counselors, providing therapy to the dis-tressed. They were problem-solvers. But in their shift in social status from a group identified with the aspirations of the poor, and therefore basically anti-establishment, to a group acting for that establishment, or at least blessed by it, they lost a great deal of their zeal for changing society, either one by one or by social activism. They became more concerned about upholding professional standards, and about their techniques. They wanted to select their clients and the problems that they worked on, rather than meet need where they found it. An article on "insight therapy" makes both of these points,[30] and the internecine war between the followers of Rank and Freud raised more indignation than did even the administration's ban-ning of Charlotte Towle's *Common Human Needs*, or Eisen-hower's replacement of Jane Hoey as head of the Public Assistance Bureau (although some social workers protested these quite vigorously). Social work became, in fact, ingrown.

In 1962 the profession made its greatest mistake. It persuaded Congress that if more money were put into social services, the rising relief rolls could be cut substantially. Yet in a period of six years, the number of people on relief doubled. This was not social work's fault. What had come into being was the country's, and the government's, recognition of the extent of poverty in this country, and the rights movements that sprang up at the time. Specifically what swelled the rolls was that welfare recipients, through the Community Action and Legal Services programs that were part of President Johnson's War on Poverty, and through the National Welfare Rights Organization and its local counterparts, discovered what their legal rights were. They had been subjected for a long time to a multiplicity of rules and regulations, enshrined in manuals that the recipient never saw. They had been individualized to a point which, as two lawyers said, "invites arbitrary and whimsical exercises of power" and "renders it impossible for the recipient to determine himself to what he is entitled."[31] But now these manuals were made public. Social work found itself very unpopular with the people whom it had set out to serve.

The disruption of both the 1968 and 1969 National Conferences on Social Welfare made this obvious. Welfare clients and young, untrained welfare workers, the likes of the rank-and-file who had led the way in the 1930s, shouted down speakers and on one occasion held two thousand delegates hostage, refusing to let them leave a hall until they had heard the disrupters' message. It was unwise at those meetings to admit that one had a Master of Social Work degree. The skills we had hoped would help people were viewed, not without reason, as having been used to dominate and to manipulate them.

There were three different reactions to this discovery. One group, we might call them the radicals, identified with the rights movement. They declared casework dead. The future lay with community organization. The dean of one school of social work predicted that by the year 2000, 90 percent of social work students would be committed to organization, research, and policy questions, and only ten percent to direct practice with individuals. He called for "a gradual phasing out of those professional services with roots in Nineteenth Century individualism."[32] But when social workers enrolled in the War on Poverty, they found it in other than social work hands; what they knew had little relevance to the problems of the poor or the minorities. "Social work," wrote Martin Rein, "by itself had almost nothing to contribute to the reduction of the interrelated problems of unemployment, poverty and dependency."[33] Nor could it provide leadership. It had been involved so long in treatment of the sick that it did not know how to work with the essentially well. Social workers joined movements, but their activities were "marginal to their professional tasks."[34] Although the War on Poverty proclaimed a principle which should have been most acceptable to social workers, who were still paying tribute to the concept of client self-determination, when it adopted the slogan of Maximum Feasible Participation of the poor in schemes for their betterment, and Anita Faatz called on them to use their knowledge of the helping process to help people make full use of the opportunities that were opening up for them,[35] many social workers saw more future in disruptive tactics, which they learned from political rather than social work leaders. Present structures, specifically welfare departments, were to be abolished. As one worker put it, "It is through the process of making the individual dependent, insecure, intimidated, unsafe and the like that the welfare department unwittingly arrives towards what has become its main function: the destruction of dignity and self-respect."[36] Another wrote of the "awful choice" between "working through institutions they believe may be unable to overcome social rot and participating in their destruction."[37]

In addition, social workers found themselves all too often less effective than the many "indigenous workers" who were recruited at that time. One writer questioned whether in the future there would be jobs for professional social workers.[38]

This movement died with the end of the Vietnam War, with the election of President Nixon in 1968, and with the backlash against the development of informal groups which often sued local governments on behalf of the poor. Neighborhood organizations were not, in many ways, unlike the soviets which had seized power from local and state government in the Russian

Revolution. The War on Poverty was a reflection of the mood of the 1960s, and left very little permanent effect on social work and welfare policy. Few traces of it can be found today—the separation of services from eligibility for relief, quietly being reversed; the abolition of certain restrictive practices in public assistance, largely through court decisions. It was, perhaps, the last time that many social workers put their ideals before their professional concerns, although their idealism was not always altruistic. When social work students at one school formed a Social Work Action Group, it was not in an effort to reform society, but to insist on the rights of students and of women in the profession.

A second group still clung to casework, but believed that it had failed. That it had failed to do something that it never should have been called on to do—to change human behavior, to produce what an earlier writer had called "more personally and socially effective or satisfactory behavior,"[39] with emphasis on the word "satisfactory"—was not the point. Articles began to appear claiming that, in the words of one writer, casework had "failed to demonstrate that it is effective" and indeed "lack of effectiveness appears to be the rule rather than the exception across several categories of clients, problems, situations and types of casework."[40]

Few people asked, effective for what? Casework, perhaps America's proudest invention in the field of social work, had to be made to work, or social work would cease to exist. It had not been scientific enough. The result was the so-called Knowledge Explosion and a tremendous emphasis on research. Casework, critics argued, had been too dependent on psychoanalytic theory. It needed to incorporate the findings of anthropology, learning theory, epidemiology, economics, organizational management, and a host of other sciences. These, it may be remarked, are all "external" sciences. With many workers' abandonment of psychoanalysis as ineffective, the "from the inside out" orientation, which had been the source of so much solidarity between worker and client, was lost. So was much of Freud's emphasis on relationships.

There is, I think, some question as to how much useful new knowledge the Knowledge Explosion actually provided the worker in the field. Research, particularly "outcome" research, was useful in social work's new concern with accountability, a natural result of its apparent failure. But research could for the most part measure only certain rather crude outcomes, mostly of a behavioral nature, thus strengthening social work's belief in its mission as a regulatory profession in the interests of the culture. Results that could not be measured were held to be illusory, even those measured by client satisfaction, since these were not replicable.[41] When Joel Fischer declared a "quiet revolution" in social work, in which social workers would give up their "vague" reliance on theories and tradition in favor of those models shown to be effective, he predicted that they would use behavior modification and cognitive change procedures. Both are essentially manipulative techniques. Genuineness, empathy, and warmth were accorded some validity, "although not so elegant and consistent."[42] The "new breed" of social worker will be a "scientific practitioner" researching as he or she practices, although it is a little hard to see how one can scientifically employ genuineness.

Being a scientific practitioner and a researcher, it might be noted, is much more academically respectable than merely being a caseworker. Although graduate schools of social work still trained mostly clinical personnel, the faculty were for the most part D.S.W.'s and Ph.D.'s who published or perished. Academic excellence rather than practical wisdom or a sense of mission became the criteria for success. Professional periodicals largely published research studies, and any new idea or concept had to be researched before it could be adopted. This academicism would seem to inhibit a good deal of innovation and experimentation, even where these might seem logical and useful.

A third group, which somewhat overlapped the second, in that some of its members accepted the "new" knowledge, were those who abandoned the social services and set themselves up in private practice. To them the word "social" ceased to have anything to do with society as a whole—it meant only that they took societal factors into consideration as they diagnosed and treated their clients. Otherwise, it would be hard to see them as social workers.

It is not in any way suggested that they lacked empathy for their clients, or did not serve their clients' needs. Indeed, the opportunity to meet needs without limitations of agency policy and finances is said to be one of the factors encouraging private practice.[43] So is continuing direct contact with clients as the social worker becomes more experienced and would, in an agency structure, normally be promoted to a supervisory or administrative position. Private practitioners tend to be very experienced and very skilled workers. They are also said to be the most financially ambitious. The fact remains that private practice requires a clientele with the ability to pay for service. The quest to have insurance coverage for the less well-to-do may represent a desire to enhance income as much as a commitment to the poor.

Private practitioners, along with other clinical social workers, have led the battle for state licensing of the profession, and for a higher level of accreditation of themselves and other clinicians. Again, there can be two motives. One is concern that people with inadequate skills and preparation might attempt inappropriate treatment, the other is a desire to eliminate unauthorized competition. This is normal in any profession—witness medicine and the law—but preoccupation with licensing, accreditation, and standards can easily obscure mission.

One must, I think, question whether a profession that claims to be socially sanctioned, that treats its clients as objects of research (or is urged to do so because that research will ultimately benefit all clients), that measures results largely in terms of behavioral change, that has virtually abandoned the poor, that is struggling to become licensed, and that has seen many of its most skilled workers enter the business world, can do much to ameliorate society or further true democracy. What would cause these changes, other than matters on which most social workers have little impact—structural changes, better education, economic reform, and greater social benefits—is not so much the treatment of the mentally ill or the solving of personal problems by expert counselors, but guaranteeing that the growing underclass should be treated with equity and dignity, as full citizens of their community and their nation. What they need more than anything is hope, and social workers are the potential messengers of that hope. Yet increasingly social work has left this task to untrained workers, hampered by almost intolerable burdens of regulations. In addition, a deeply suspicious bureaucracy is concerned more about someone getting help to which he or she is not entitled than about helping someone who is in desperate need. By and large these workers have done a pretty good job and have prevented further alienation, particularly in rural areas. They have shown, as Dr. Frankwood Williams said of social workers in the 1930s and 1940s, "a high statistical incidence of decency."[44] But they have had little help from the leaders of their profession, to whom they might reasonably look for inspiration.

It would be idle to suggest that social work should drop its professional aspirations, which have much good in them if they are not pushed to the extreme, or that social work should rediscover the virtue of humility. Neither humanism nor positivism has any use for this virtue. Nor, one might say, has our economic system. Social workers are products of their time and of their culture. In the last forty years, America has not had much sense of solidarity, a virtue defined as "a collective responsibility for the fate of each individual" which is "ultimately incompatible with the dynamics of a capitalist market system."[45] It essence is perhaps best illustrated by Eugene Debs's well-known statement, "While there is a man in prison, I am not free."

It is fruitless, however, to repine or to apportion blame. It would be much more sensible to try to see what there is in the present situation to indicate possible change. There may, of course, be changes that have nothing to do with social work itself—swings of the political pendulum, another depression, or a war short of total destruction—changes which tend to pull people together. But there are also tendencies within social work itself which offer a base for change. Ever since Mary Richmond discovered, as a pragmatic principle, that "the fullest possible participation of the client in all plans" was one of the three most successful policies in social work—the others are stimulation, encouragement, and the skillful use of repetition—and developed what she called the principle of client self-determination,[46] social workers have recognized this principle as an essential part of their philosophy. The principle has been much limited, even denied to certain groups, such as unmarried mothers in respect to their babies.[47] At times it has been put in the form of "I believe in self-determination but . . . ," reduced from king to citizen in the realm of social work values,[48] and not fostered or accorded as a right.[49] Despite all that, the field has never altogether abandoned it. In its sense of client participation it has been revived by the enlarged use of contracts in private practice.

There is also some indication that many social workers are becoming a little uneasy with the confines of Cartesian science. Dialogue with religious thinkers is more common. *Social Casework,* the most clinical of social work's major periodicals, has published in the last seven years two articles with specific religious content.[50] The effect of the proliferation of B.S.W. programs in church-sponsored colleges and seminaries—now one-third of all accredited undergraduate programs—on the field will be interesting to see. These students have a mission: some seek true solidarity with the poor and a sense of common human vulnerability, while others tend to be moralistic or evangelistic. My teaching experience at one such school, one supposed to be very conservative, gives me reason to hope.

There are, I believe, two models which the profession might consider if it wishes to regain a sense of mission. Both have to do with an approach to people who need our help. One which I tried to promote in the early 1970s might be called "co-planning."[51] I went so far as to suggest it as an answer to the question asked by Reid and others, "What do social workers do?," but this suggestion was too controversial.[52] The concept is enhanced if one believes that in this post-industrial age everyone, not only the disadvantaged or the maladjusted, needs help in coping with the complexities of modern life, help in dealing with organizations, in playing social roles for which one was not educated (single parent, retiree, welfare client, for example), or in choosing a lifestyle. Such assistance can become "routine, necessary and universal."[53]

Co-planning, which is applicable to work with individuals, groups, community organizations, and to consultation with agencies or organizations, starts with the assumption that the person or body needing help is normally competent, but is ambivalent, confused, overwhelmed, angry, defeated, acting illogically or without sufficient knowledge—this is not intended as a complete list—to some circumstances in their life. The basic questions co-planning asks are, "Now that this has happened or you face this problem, what do you want to do about it?" "Can you do it?" "Will that really satisfy you?" "What help will you need to do it?" It does not deny the need for psychotherapy—indeed, psychotherapy may be what a person needs and, thus, be part of the plan—but it does not start with the assumption that psychotherapy is needed. In some way the process can be compared to what a travel agent does, done in the areas of social services, social roles, and social institutions. One does not tell someone where to go, but helps him, her, or them find the most practical and possibly the least costly way to get there.

But even more, American social work can look at the development in the United Kingdom of what is known as Community Social Work (not to be confused with Community Organization as taught and practiced in America). In Community Social Work, social workers, instead of "intervening"—a social work term dating back only to the 1960s, and implying action from the outside—actually become part of the community with which they are working and "look for a way of working simultaneously at both the individual and community levels."[54] It attempts not only to help with an individual's problem but, by helping, to create the resources that will build a community able to resolve similar problems. It smacks a little of the indigenous worker, but an indigenous worker with social work skills. It may involve actions very foreign to American social work, such as solving some of one community's problems by helping it establish a neighborhood laundry. But perhaps the most significant contribution Community Social Work has made to social work theory is its removal of the people with whom the worker works from the category of "clients" seeking help from an expert. Instead, these people become co-workers, or "constituents."

This work has a strong moral purpose, a commitment to the public good and a mission that is not necessarily religious; it may, in fact, in Britain be socialist in origin, or be informed by a sense of solidarity. It is very far from being self-seeking. Its ultimate goal, the same as that of co-planning, is a more open and just, and less oppressive society. Recent action by the Clark/Atlanta University School of Social Work, whose faculty (including the dean) and students elected to live in the area with the greatest social problems, shows something of this spirit.

There is certainly a need for psychotherapists and clinicians in our society, and there is no reason why these should not work in private practice or agitate for professional recognition and rewards. But I wish they would stop calling themselves "social workers," or that those who act from an entirely different motivation—those really concerned with the quality of life accorded the most vulnerable in our society, those called to do something about it and prepared not only to learn but to acquire the self-discipline needed to serve society—could find themselves another name.

Notes

1. Esther Gabriel, "Private Practice in Social Work," *Encyclopedia of Social Work*, 17th ed. (Silver Spring, Md.: NASW, 1977), 1054.

2. Lionel Trilling, *Freud and the Crisis of Our Culture* (Boston: Beacon Press, 1955), 48.

3. Bertha Reynolds, "Re-Thinking Social Case Work," *Social Work Today* 5 (April–June 1938): 15.

4. Allen F. Davis, *Spearheads for Reform: The Social Settlements and the Progressive Movement, 1890–1914* (New York: Oxford University Press, 1967), 34–35.

5. Bertha M. Kraus, "The Role of Social Case Work in American Social Work," in Cora Kasius, ed., *Principles and Techniques in Social Case Work* (New York: Family Service Association of America, 1950), 139.

6. Alan Keith-Lucas, *Giving and Taking Help* (Chapel Hill, N.C.: University of North Carolina Press, 1972), 136ff.

7. Nevil Masterman, ed., *Chalmers on Charity: A Selection of Passages and Themes to Illustrate the Social Teaching and Practical Work of Thomas Chalmers, D.D.* (Westminster, England: A. Constable & Company, 1900), 124.

8. D. O. Kellogg, "The Principle Advantage of Association in Charity," reprinted in Ralph E. Pumphrey and Muriel W. Pumphrey, eds., *The Heritage of American Social Work* (New York: Columbia University Press, 1961), 174–75.

9. James A. Bonaparte, "The Ethics of Organized Charity," reprinted in Pumphrey and Pumphrey, eds., *The Heritage*, 191.

10. Jane Addams, "The Subtle Problems of Charity," reprinted in *The Heritage*, 275.

11. Mary Richmond, "The Need for a Training School in Applied Philanthropy," 1897. Reprinted in *The Heritage*, 291.

12. Jeffrey M. Masson, "Freud and the Seduction Theory," *Atlantic Monthly* (February 1984): 33–59.

13. Philip S. Klein, "Social Work: Social Casework," *Encyclopedia of the Social Sciences*, vol. 14 (New York: Macmillan & Company, 1950), 178.

14. Dorothy Kahn, "Democratic Principles in Public Assistance," *Proceedings of the National Conference of Social Work* (New York: Columbia University Press, 1939), 275–76.

15. Gordon Hamilton, "The Underlying Philosophy of Social Casework," in Kasius, *Principles and Techniques*, 10.

16. Elizabeth Saloman, "Humanistic Values and Social Casework," *Social Casework* 48 (January 1967): 27.

17. Gordon Hamilton, "Basic Concepts in Social Work," in Fern Lowry, ed., *Readings in Social Casework, 1920–38* (New York: Columbia University Press, 1939), 156. Quotes from Ruth Benedict, *Patterns of Culture* (Boston and New York: Houghton Mifflin Company, 1934), 258.

18. Ruth Ellen Lindenberg, "Hard to Reach: Client or Casework Agency?" *Social Work* 3 (October 1958): 29.

19. Reynolds, "Re-Thinking Social Case Work," 15.

20. Eda Houwick, *The Place of Case Work in a Public Assistance Program* (Chicago: American Public Welfare Association, 1941), 8–9.

21. Elliot Studt, "An Outline for Study of Social Authority Factors in Casework," *Social Casework* 35 (June 1954): 232.

22. Robert E. Taylor, "The Social Control Function in Social Work," *Social Casework* 39 (1958): 17–21.

23. Jeanette Regensburg, "Reaching Children Before the Crisis Comes," *Social Casework* 35 (1954): 106.

24. A. Delafield Smith, "Community Prerogative and the Legal Rights and Freedom of the Individual," *Social Security Bulletin* (August 1946): 6.

25. Alvin Schorr, "The Tendency to R_x," *Social Work* 7 (January 1962): 59–66.

26. Gordon Hamilton, "The Role of Social Casework in Social Policy," in National Conference of Social Work, *Selected Papers in Casework, 1952* (New York: Columbia University Press, 1953), 71.

27. Rudolph Dansted, "A Possibility for Social Rehabilitation," *Public Welfare* 7 (April 1952): 47.

28. Kermit Wiltse, "Social Casework Services in the Aid to Dependent Children Program," *Social Service Review* 28 (1954): 176.

29. Werner Boehm, "Casework: A Psychosocial Therapy," *Child Welfare* 43 (1964): 535–8.

30. Lucille Austin, "Trends in Differential Treatment in Social Casework," in Kasius, *Principles and Techniques*, 337.

31. Jacobus ten Broek and Richard B. Wilson, "Public Assistance and Social Insurance: A Normative Evaluation," *U.C.L.A. Law Review* 2 (1954): 2-5-56.

32. Alan D. Wade, quoted in Mary Gyafasa, "Social Science Technology and Social Work," *Social Service Review 43* (1969): 266.

33. Martin Rein, "Social Work in Search of a Radical Profession," *Social Work* 15 (April 1970): 17.

34. Ibid., 28.

35. Anita Faatz, "Social Work and the Poverty Program," Isabelle K. Carter Lecture, University of North Carolina, 1965.

36. Martin Eisman, "Social Work's New Role in the Welfare Class Revolution," *Social Work* 14 (April 1969): 81.

37. Harry Specht, "Disruptive Tactics," *Social Work* 14 (April 1969): 14.

38. Harry Specht, "The Deprofessionalization of Social Work," *Social Work* 17 (April 1972): 17.

39. Wiltse, "Social Casework Services," 178.

40. Joel Fischer, "Is Casework Effective?—A Review," *Social Work* 18 (January 1973): 9.

41. Edward Newman and Jerry Turem, "The Crisis of Accountability," *Social Work* 19 (January 1974): 6.

42. Joel Fischer, "The Social Work Revolution," *Social Work* 26 (May 1981): 205.

43. Gabriel, "Private Practice," 1054.

44. Quoted by Gertrude Springer, "The Responsibility of a Social Worker in a Democracy," *Proceedings of the National Conference of Social Work* (New York: Columbia University Press, 1942), 65.

45. Gosta Esping-Andersoen, "After the Welfare State," *Public Welfare* 41 (Winter 1983): 28.

46. Mary Richmond, *What Is Social Case Work?* (New York: Russell Sage Foundation, 1922), 256.

47. Dorothy Hutchinson, "Re-examination of Some Aspects of Case Work Practice in Adoption," *Child Welfare League of America Bulletin* (November 1946): 6.

48. Saul Bernstein, "Self-Determination: King or Citizen in the Realm of Social Work Values," *Social Work* 5 (January 1960): 3–8.

49. "Code of Ethics of the National Association of Social Workers," in *Encyclopedia of Social Work*, 18th ed. (Silver Spring, Md.: NASW, 1987), 951–56.

50. Diana M. Meystedt, "Religion and the Rural Population: Implications for Social Work," *Social Casework 65* (1984): 219–25. Edward

R. Canda, "Spirituality, Religious Diversity and Social Work Practice," *Social Casework* 69 (April 1988): 238–47.

51. Alan Keith-Lucas, "Philosophies of Public Service," *Public Welfare* 31 (1973): 21–24.

52. Alan Keith Lucas, in a paper rejected by *Social Work* in 1970. The material was considered too controversial for publication.

53. Edward R. Lowenstein, "Social Work in a Post-Industrial Society," *Social Work* 18 (November 1973): 47.

54. David W. Harrison, "Reflective Practice in Social Care," *Social Service Review* 66 (1987): 343–404.

CHAPTER FIVE

Strengthening the Moral Mission of Social Work

Max Siporin

A cynical fashion observer remarked that currently in our society: "Morality is In, Immortality is Out." There may be some truth in this observation, although we trust that what is happening is not a fashion or a fad. It is true is that there are historical cycles, and that we appear to be on the upswing of a new cultural era in regard to morality. For several years now a veritable social movement has been under way toward stricter standards of moral conduct. There is a revival of religious, spiritual consciousness and practice. The "anything goes" mood of the 1960s and 1970s is definitely over; higher standards of moral and ethical behavior are not only acceptable, but are actually being enforced. The numbers of public officials being prosecuted for wrongdoing may well be greater than in any previous era. A moral reformist approach to the resolution of social problems is now ascendent.

One can question, however, whether general rates of deviant behavior have actually declined, in view of the prevailing high incidence of drug addiction, venereal disease, and interpersonal violence. Family disorganization, poverty, and homelessness remain endemic for a significant segment of society, and these social problems are breeding grounds for greater alienation and deviance. The social reforms enacted in recent decades have not worked well in view of the growth of an underclass and an increase in the number of people living in poverty.

During the turbulent past decades the societal tasks accepted by social work have changed several times. The moral mission of social work, which is at the heart of the societal task of helping people in distress, has undergone severe modifications and appears now to be in a confused and weakened condition. We will here examine the nature of this moral mission, and how its conception has changed within the profession. In accord with the analyses in this book by Wilma Peebles-Wilkins and Beverly Koerin, and by Frederic G. Reamer, we will briefly consider how recent social changes have adversely affected social work morality. Our major purposes are to identify several tasks that are indicated to strengthen social work's moral mission, and to identify several issues that must be dealt with in accomplishing this objective.

The Moral Mission of Social Work

The profession of social work has its roots in the religious traditions and practice of charity.[1] In the new secular institutions that came into being in response to the Industrial Revolution, early social work was known as charity work. Charity work was undertaken largely by "Charity Organization Societies, and the person who provided such help was known as a charity worker. One of the first texts used to educate people for the new occupation of social work, and to aid in operating charitable programs and organizations, was Edward Devine's *The Practice of Charity*, published in 1901.[2] He described charity as "the means by which a countless number of individuals are rescued from ignorance, destitution and crime"; it "includes what one individual does for the benefit of another and what the community, through its public and private institutions and societies, does for the poor." Charity, said Charles Loch, "is social love, and that action of which social love is an expression."[3]

The early charity workers felt called to the "service ideal," and they believed that they were serving God in their service to poor, disabled, and wayward people, the "dependent, defectives and delinquents" of that time, and in their efforts to "prevent crime and pauperism."[4] Religious moral values and precepts that were altruistic and humanitarian in nature carried over into secular charity practice. Friendly visiting, the early form of casework or therapy, sought to provide a personal helping relationship and spiritual influence through which individuals and families were taught the adaptive behaviors of industry and thrift, self-reliance and self-support. The workers also organized and provided needed social resources to support such goals.

"Not alms but a friend" was the motto of the early Charity Organization Societies, which were intent on avoiding the "noxious charity" that "pauperized" the poor. The helping impulse expressed a moral concern to redeem and elevate the poor, and to help them overcome their defects in moral character. This impulse often included a moralistic zeal, as Peebles-Wilkins and Koerin indicate, that was paternalistic, authoritarian, and rejecting of the "unworthy" poor, who were either improperly motivated or unaccepting of the ministrations of the charitable helpers.

The charity workers formulated valuable understandings and precepts to guide their work. A fundamental principle was to help "rationally" and "scientifically," pursuing a study and treatment that was comprehensive, individualized, with consideration for the whole family and for the causes of their distress. They believed strongly that personal virtue (as an exercise of highly valued moral/ethical behavior) is a basic necessity for individual and community well-being. This belief yielded another basic principle of helping: Not only to relieve distress, but also to develop virtuous character and behavior, as well as a spiritual awakening that would prevent the poor, disabled, or aged from turning or returning to the deviant behavior of crime or the dependency of pauperism.[5] These beliefs expressed a new redemptive impulse to "save" human souls, for the sake not of a heavenly afterlife but of a virtuous, self-fulfilling life on earth.

Social work represented a major transformation of a moral, social consciousness and a social ethic of mutual aid, which led to the welfare state. This was based on the notion of a public, secular community responsibility for the well-being of its citizens, and another new belief that poverty was preventable. The charity workers led to the development of a new societal consciousness about poverty.[6] Poor people came to be viewed not as unworthy sinners, but as victims of societal conditions that lead to social dependency and crime. As part of such a cultural transformation, there was also a shift in viewing charity work not only as a service to God, sanctioned by religious beliefs, but as a secular, professional "service to humanity."[7] This led to a redefinition of charity work as professional social work. We should note that the secularization of social work took place within an emerging structure of welfare services, in which a substantial portion of social services continued to be provided by religious institutions; this provision continues at the present time.

The charity workers sought to help people become good, responsible, productive citizens and to help society become a good, responsible, nurturing community. In popular images of charity workers and later of social workers, they were categorized as Good Samaritans, do-gooders, and bleeding hearts, sometimes over-zealous and rigidly moralistic. They were also seen as altruistic public servants, honest, trustworthy, of moral integrity and high moral/ethical standards and ideals. They manifested a moral passion in their service to people, yet they served as exemplars of deep tolerance and acceptance of human beings, an acceptance that enfolded all members of the community, however different and wayward they might be.

Charity workers were expected to, and did, exemplify the moral character they were enjoined to teach and persuade their clients to develop. Tuckerman, a social work pioneer, declared that the aim of friendly visiting to the poor was "to extend virtue," and this was to be accomplished by the friendly visitor's "exercise of virtue."[8] The expectation by the public and the profession that the professional social worker should be a person of virtue is still alive, and is stated as an obligation in the profession's code of ethics. In a recent statement, Charles S. Levy declared, "Social workers, by virtue of the work that they are assigned or assumed to do, and are sanctioned by the community to do, and by virtue of the relationships which that work requires, are committed to, and expected to live and act by, a morality that is relevant to that work."[9]

This kind of public image and self-image gave social workers a moral authority that enhanced their influence with clients and with the public, making for a general acceptance of social work purposes and procedures.

Evolution of the Moral Mission

With years of experience in helping casualties of the new industrial society, and as a consequence of the great economic depression of the 1890s, social workers came to understand first, that, society often provokes the social and moral conflicts, problems, and dilemmas that cause its distress, and second, society often does not provide the resources people need to develop and function well. Social workers did not accept the function, which some sponsors sought to impose, of staving off a radical socio-economic revolution. The term "charity" came to be viewed as discordant with the idea of community responsibility to aid fellow citizens for the common good.

"Justice, not Charity" became the battle cry of the social reformers who sought to expand public and private provisions of relief to the unemployed and the poor, and also to change social conditions to eliminate poverty and other social problems.[10] Devine spoke of charity as "relief" and as "enlightened relief policy" in aid to the poor, "of a kind that will transform the unfit into such as are fit to survive, and . . . may alter the conditions which create the unfit."[11] Around the turn of the century, the social reform impulse led social workers to an activism that helped change negative community attitudes toward poverty, organized the community to provide needed resources to those in want, and helped enact legislative reforms at local, state, and national levels of government.

Another development was a shift in social work thinking to a more humanitarian, democratic ethos, away from the early paternalistic moralism. The charity agents and "friendly visitors" came to be guided by ethical principles of empathic caring, of acceptance of people as inherently worthy. In time the subjects of charity came to be understood as fellow human beings with common human needs. Still later the clients of social work were understood to have inalienable human rights to a decent standard of living, health, liberty, and the social resources needed for a decent standard of development and functioning. Great value was increasingly placed on individual differences and choice, which meant tolerance of different lifestyles, and was expressed in the formulation of ethical practice principles of respect for client self-determination, and for client participation in decisions affecting his or her welfare.

In becoming professionals, paid by the community and serving as its moral caretaking agents, social workers fulfilled a social contract to be of benefit to people in need. Social work no longer needed to be seen as a way of achieving divine grace or earning a heavenly reward. Rather, it expressed the community's public, social responsibility for the common welfare of its citizens. By formalizing the social contract, social work became a community function, while continuing as a cause of social reform and a calling for those who desired to be of service to others. This social contract is now formalized through legal licensing of social work and official accreditation of social work educational programs.

The early social reform movement within the new profession of social work thus influenced further changes in the understanding of social work's mission in society. The new social workers accepted societal responsibility for a two-fold approach in helping to relieve and prevent problems of deviance and dependency. The first part of this approach was to help individuals and families to function optimally; the second was to help modify situational, social-structural, institutional, and community arrangements to support such optimum functioning.[12] The emphasis on coordinating charitable efforts evolved from a concern with avoiding giving indiscriminate help into a plan for developing programs for community organization and social action. Along with family and individual helping activities, the problem-person-situation approach was a comprehensive attack on the causes of dependency and deviance.

This two-fold function led social workers to assume leadership roles in the development and administration of the social welfare institution; they became its central profession, and remain so today. Social workers have also assumed the tasks of aiding social integration and promoting social order in the community to support this integration, which has meant helping people of different social groups establish mutually supportive relationships with respect for human diversity. Another task-function is to mediate between individuals and families and their social institutions for complementary, reciprocal relationships, advocate for the disadvantaged, and encourage a cohesive, democratic, just society. Thus, social work is called upon to serve as an instrument of both social change and social stability, or control, and to help balance these polarities of the dynamic societal process.[13]

The mission of social work to help relieve dependency and deviance is primarily a moral one: To help people live rightly, for their own and for the collective good. Social work is therefore a moral, normative discipline, aiding people to become or remain responsible, rational, moral agents; to deal with their value conflicts and moral choices concerning good and evil; and to avoid or cope with the consequences of their deviant behavior.[14] Helping to realize a good, just society through social reform also has a moral character. The explicit value system is a central feature of social work as a professional practice; it continues to give social work a distinctive social identity as a helping profession. In the methods and processes of practice it uses to achieve social and moral objectives, social work is also a scientific art.

The social work profession accepted its societal functions and tasks as a foundation for the development of a two-fold base for professional practice, that of a philosophy and a body of knowledge. Upon this base, social workers have developed a helping method of practice. The philosophy is primary, formulated in terms of a moral system and ideology, and translated into a set of ethical practice principles. The problem-person-situation model of social work practice actualizes basic social work values: Human worth and dignity; individuality and diversity; complementarity, interdependence, reciprocity, and mutual aid; caring (or acceptance), social responsibility and justice. Hughes suggests that these values derive from "natural law," and represent "natural virtues."[15] The virtues, he says, are the essence of individual and collective humanity, and could provide a common moral ground for social workers.

Such an understanding of the social work mission was jointly formulated by society and by social workers themselves. The social contract between the profession and society may exist in ambiguous terms and, as Reid argues in chapter 3, the responsibility and social authority for the tasks involved have not been fully granted by society, nor is society clear about how accountability is to be fulfilled. On balance, however, society has granted the profession a great deal of financial support and legal recognition, which sanction social work functions and responsibilities.

Moral Theory as Base of the Moral Mission

In accepting their assignments to serve as moral agents of society and to carry out the task-functions identified above, social workers formulated a moral theory as a base for the profession's ethical practice principles. The moral theory has been neither well, nor fully, nor explicitly formulated and the profession has not thoroughly digested its interdisciplinary borrowings from philosophy or psychology. Still, the moral theory is clearly identifiable and, until recently, had a consensual acceptance within the profession.

There are, of course, points of difference among social workers about this moral philosophy and its theoretical rationale. Some social workers misunderstand and reject the idea that they serve as moral agents of the community. They may believe this means they must serve the regulatory, repressive status-quo; they may equate morality with paternalism or religious moralism; they may prefer to see themselves as tolerantly and scientifically value-free toward clients; they may believe that being nonjudgmental of people also means being nonjudgmental of their behavior. It is therefore helpful to clarify this moral/ethical system of ideas and its rationale.

The moral theory presents several assumptions or behavior principles, as part of its rationale.[16] Human beings organize, choose, and justify their behavior in terms of their values and of the norms and standards upon which these values are based. Morality consists of choice between right and wrong values, and of action based on that choice, even though situational factors greatly influence the actual decision and the action that results. Value commitments are associated with the internalization of moral values as part of the person's conscience and character; they become a source of moral energy, and justification for moral/ethical conduct. Virtue represents the capacity for implementation of these values in moral/ethical conduct to some excellent degree. Laws, mores, and customs are the institutionalized values of a community. Immoral behavior is harmful conduct that is deviant from community values and norms, though such misbehavior may have progressive, beneficial purposes and consequences.

A basic article of social work faith is a belief in the necessity for principled ethical conduct in human relationships. Normative, that is, morally right, socially acceptable, behavior enables trust, intimacy, love, integration, empathy, reciprocity, and collaboration in democratic, transactional relationships with others for the common good. Such normative relationships also enable self-development and self-realization, since self-development and individuality require social interdependence and reciprocity to secure needed resources, whether love or food. Individual and social welfare are thus essentially interwoven and interdependent, requiring a positive complementarity of strengths and deficiencies, resources and restraints. Similarly, the dysfunctioning of an individual and his or her community are interdependent and mutually reinforcing, resulting in mutual harm.

The inherent human need for spiritual meaning, experience, and growth is also met by principled relations between people and with ultimate reality, which some people call God. Spirituality has a basic moral meaning, in an individual's search for what is good and avoidance of evil or vice. There is also a moral meaning in the spiritual pursuit of right (normative) paths to a wholeness of self-realization and an authentic identity, as well as to self-transcendence, epiphany, and grace. These objectives may be sought in religious or nonreligious contexts.

Society and its governments assume responsibility for developing and maintaining the moral character of its members, and for inculcating in them consciences, moral values, ethical precepts, and habits of ethical behavior and relationships. The family has an important function in socializing its members to develop personal moralities that are adaptive for their culture. Many social workers of a libertarian persuasion accept the necessity for governmental provisions to regulate individual behavior, in order to maintain social cohesion and moral order for the common good. At issue, though, is the extent to which laws should prescribe, proscribe, tolerate, or discourage specific conduct.

In the development of this moral theory, social workers adopted the set of basic values from which they have derived ethical practice principles. For example, the inherent worth of the individual is a primary social work value, and respect for this quality of clients is a primary ethical practice principle.

The social work value system contains a number of "both-and" sets of moral values, such as the link of caring (or charity, caritas, chesed, or sadaqah) with justice (or fair, equitable treatment in terms of reward and punishment).[17] Caring and justice are also tied to the value of competence, in making judgments and providing services that assure constructive results.

Social work ethical practice principles are stated in the profession's Code of Ethics.[18] The code pertains to the social worker's own conduct, as well as to relationships with clients, colleagues, employers, the social work profession, and society in general. It tells practitioners for example, that, "The social worker should regard as primary the service obligations of the social work profession . . . should maintain high standards of personal conduct in the capacity or identity as a social worker . . . should not exploit professional relationships for personal gain." The manipulation or sexual exploitation of clients are forms of unethical conduct in violation of this code. The profession's formulation and adoption of such a code was actuated, in part, by a desire for societal recognition of its professional status, on the assumption that a real profession has an explicit, publicly adopted, and sanctioned code of ethics. But the Code of Ethics also represents a formulation of ethical obligations to use as practical principles. These precepts are extremely useful in guiding social work practitioners, helping them deal with the very complex moral/ethical problems at the core of their practice.

Social workers are asked to help clients with difficult moral/ethical dilemmas and conflicts, and to cope with such issues in their own lives. Much good work has been done to help practitioners with these dilemmas.[19] However, the ethical principles help with these decision tasks only to a limited degree; beyond that, situations often require the application of discretionary judgment to complex circumstances. Such burdens add to the stresses that are a prominent feature of social work.

Reamer observes that "applications of core values in social work have undergone substantial change over the years in response to social, political, and economic developments," but the core values themselves have remained stable.[20] The emphasis on specific values and principles, and on their interpretations—for example, about self-determination—has shifted with time, yet social workers have maintained their commitment to these fundamental values.

In recent research, Ann A. Abbott confirmed this continued commitment. She found that social work students, faculty members, and seasoned practitioners are different from other professionals in their value beliefs.[21] As a professional group they are more liberal, "more aware of their social responsibility to promote the well-being of others, and are more active in fulfilling that responsibility"; they believe in "the importance of individual freedom and of encouraging individual choice (self-determination)"; and they are concerned about cultural diversity, women's issues, institutional oppression, and societal injustice.

Social Changes and Their Effects

The societal functions of social work as a profession have changed in the face of vast socio-economic and demographic changes during recent decades. The tasks of helping people to function optimally, and of dealing with problems of dependency and deviant behavior, remain viable. To this observer, they now appear more specific and realistic. Some of the changes that have altered social work tasks are constructive and others are not.

Social trends that have altered the moral mission and societal task-functions of social work include the counter-cultural, anti-war, civil rights, and women's movements, along with a renewed mental health crusade. All these trends influenced what came to be termed in the 1960s a "moral revolution."

The moral revolution involved acceptance of an individualistic, materialistic, relativistic ethos and value system within our modern culture.[22] Primacy was given to values of individual self-fulfillment and autonomy, largely separated from social authority structures and from values of the common good and the collective welfare of the community. Self-fulfillment is not viewed as based on social interdependence, responsibility, and reciprocity. Moral relativism, libertarianism, and egoism became fashionable, as did rejection of certain traditional values, behavioral norms, and moral concepts. The terms "immorality," "virtue," and "sin" became unpopular; guilt and shame were viewed as unnecessary and even harmful feelings. Although certain specifics are still a matter of some controversy, a wide range of deviant behavior and lifestyles were considered nondeviant for a culturally diverse society, and open to free choice. These attitudes, in part, involve an anti-religious bias, and many traditional moral standards are rejected because they are associated with restrictive religious dogma and practices.

Contributing to a moral libertarianism are scientific and mental health ideologies widely adopted within social work. We went through a period, in the 1950s and 1960s, when a positivistic scientific approach was interpreted as a value-free orientation, and was applied to bolster claims for the acceptance of a scientific social work. The mental health ethic, of which psychoanalytic psychology became a part, attempted to substitute a medical model, and the concepts and psychiatric terminology of mental health and illness, for moral aspects of social functioning and dysfunction, deviant behavior, and moral/ethical problems in social living.

The National Association of Social Workers has accepted a categorization of social work as a mental health profession, so that clinical social agencies and clinical social workers are qualified for reimbursement as "mental health service providers." Therapy is the name of the main game in the helping professions today, and many social workers have flocked into private practice to do therapy.

We should note that mental health ideology was used unsuccessfully to tackle social problems through political activism in terms of community psychiatry and community mental health.[23] This medical-psychiatric, scientific cloak is often a con game, through which morally corrective objectives are covertly pursued, with doubtful success.[24] We will discuss the negative consequences for social work in a later section.

The Erosion of the Moral Mission

The course of social work history, as Mary Richmond observed, consists of spiraling cycles of attention to individual, or "retail," moral reform and to social, or "wholesale," reform.[25] While continuing to accept the profession's two-fold function, social work's responsiveness to socio-economic and cultural changes has made for an emphasis alternating between helping to create good, virtuous people and helping to create a good, just society. Thus we had social activist eras from the 1930s to the early 1940s, and again from the late 1960s to the late 1970s. Between these periods, and at present, social workers have focused more on individual and family moral reform, now termed "therapy."

With each swing of the pendulum, some social workers have exhibited excessive moral zeal, extremist dogmatism and messianism. Some true believers of each camp claimed to know the right path to utopia, have fiercely battled and scorned unbelievers, and have acted imperiously to achieve their objectives. Supposedly liberal, enlightened social workers, including some in schools of social work, have indulged in this kind of derogatory behavior. During the 1940s the diagnostic Freudians virtually shut out the Rankian functionalists in almost all schools of social work. During the 1970s the behaviorists and the social activists in many schools of social work blocked or ejected psychodynamic partisans. Some consequences of such extremisms were positive, but the hostile controversies they generated have also been counter-productive.[26]

There have been all too few critical analyses of these changes, as they relate to social work morality, in the recent literature.[27] Reamer, in chapter 2, and Alan Keith-Lucas, in chapter 4, have provided trenchant criticisms of the current trends toward professionalism and careerism, and of the withdrawal from social work's moral commitment to helping the poor and to working in public welfare.

These social and cultural changes have not only modified the moral mission of social work, they have eroded its substance. We note that the moral vision, idealism, and commitment of social work have been weakened. Social workers—at least in the popular literature—are no longer viewed as models of incorruptible, self-sacrificing virtue.[28] There are more incidents now of social worker malfeasance and corruption in public positions. Fortunately, very few social workers have been sued for malpractice, possibly because social workers are still largely believed to be committed to the service ideal.[29]

There is also an evident moral confusion on the part of a

substantial segment of social workers about what are normal, abnormal, or pathological behaviors. Avoidance of the moral nature of social work and reliance on a mental health/illness terminology obfuscate and evade direct dealings with the moral complexities of life. This evasion weakens the ability of social workers to help clients deal with moral issues.

The liberated morality has found widespread acceptance in the social work establishment of professional associations and educational institutions. This acceptance has shattered the formerly consensual value system and generated much controversy and divisiveness within the profession. Along with the increasing public acceptance of social workers for the provision of mental health services, there is a weakened authority of social workers as moral agents of the community.

Recent Trends Toward a New Moral Consciousness

The current situation is not so negative as the above analysis may suggest. Several positive trends indicate a potential for a progressive development. For example, a significant number of social workers continue to regard social work as a cause and calling, and retain their social idealism and moral commitments to service to the poor and to social reform.[30] More important, in very recent years, major socio-cultural changes have occurred to modify the moral scene, within both society and social work. These changes express a new moral consciousness. They may presage a renewal of the moral mission of social work, if we can make a concerted effort to facilitate such a process.

The present strong conservative mood of our cultural climate emerged following the counter-cultural, commune, and anti-war movements of the 1960s and the anti-poverty and civil rights movements of the 1960s and 1970s. All these movements had a common moral concern. The counter-cultural and commune movements placed a strong emphasis on right-minded ethical conduct and relationships, however misguided some of their conceptions. The civil rights and anti-poverty movements were strongly moral in their demands for fair, just treatment of minorities, women, the poor, and the disabled, even though they made unsuccessful efforts to politicize and radicalize social workers and their clients. The disappointment with, retreat from, and backlash against the extreme radicalism of the 1970s have pushed people in conservative moral directions. The evident high costs of current epidemics of venereal disease, drug addiction, and HIV (AIDS) infections, defined as the results of immoral behavior, have added fuel to this conservative trend. But at the same time, we discern an ongoing evolutionary process of a new moral/ethical sensibility.

A particularly important development is the presence within social work of the religious revival and the spiritual or New Age consciousness movement.[31] Religiously-oriented social workers have continued to constitute an important segment of the profession. Among social workers and the general public, we now see a great turning to religious beliefs and practices, a seeking for spiritual and moral experience, meaning, and relatedness. This appears to be an effort to fill the spiritual voids created by materialistic and individualistic values, as well as by the political activism of the preceding period. There are heterogeneous forms of religious practice operating in this movement, appealing to people of both institutionally religious and non-institutional persuasions. They have a common interest in experiential approaches to humanistic moral meanings and conduct, which meet spiritual needs and relate people more directly to one another and to the ultimate forces of life.

Contributing to the spirituality-consciousness movement is the existentialist philosophic thought that achieved a degree of popularity during the 1960s within the youth counter-culture, as well as within the helping professions, including social work. Its influence declined during the 1970s, but it gathered renewed strength during the 1980s. The existentialist concern for spiritual consciousness and values, for authenticity, autonomy, and self-development, expresses a striving for personal moral improvement. This has been applied in social work to mean a more conscious attention to values of individual worth, will, and honesty, and of empathic caring and kindness, personal and social responsibility.[32] Cognitive theory and constructionist ideas about how people create and interpret their reality may be understood as part of this existentialist strand of thought. Developed in philosophy, cognitive psychology, and literary theory, these theoretical approaches are being applied to social work with increasing acceptance, and are also part of a shift from positivist scientism to a humanistic scientific orientation.[33]

Toward a Renewal of the Moral Mission

Social workers have been influenced by and have contributed to these trends toward a new moral consciousness. They continue to participate, assuming leading roles, in various branches of the civil rights movement, particularly with regard to the rights of welfare clients, minorities, and women. Many have turned to religious modes of experience and to the commune and New Age spirituality movements. When these movements surfaced as moral crusades, social workers provided a predisposed, receptive, eager, and supportive constituency. The messages and meanings of these causes touched the very core of the motivations—humanitarian service and social reform—that draw people into social work.

In social work as in society, there is now a retreat from the moral libertarianism of past decades, a return to stricter moral/ethical standards for public and private conduct, and a rejection of double standards for sexual and other behavior. We observe widespread public support for the severe punishment of national, state, and local legislators and public and corporate officials who have been convicted for corruption, malfeasance, fraud, and other misconduct. There will, of course, continue to be a great deal of deviant behavior since, paradoxically, the existence of deviant behavior helps people know what is good, act rightly, and change their attitudes and circumstances so that they can continue acting rightly even in stressful and confusing situations.

We next examine a set of tasks that are indicated in our effort to renew and reshape the moral mission of social work. A set of significant issues needs to be tackled as part of this endeavor. There is a continuing question about biological, psychic, or social determinism in regard to morality and other behavior: does morality stem mostly from within the person, or primarily from socio-cultural forces? Another controversial question confronts the nature of behavior characterized as moral or immoral, deviant or normal, acceptable or intolerable and punishable; such judgments involve discretionary, complex judgments and principles. We will not address these issues here.

Instead, we will consider some additional issues of social work's moral task-functions in society, dealing with the medical-psychiatric model of therapy, and the provision of therapeutic services on a private-practice basis. We also will consider the issues of religious and nontheistic rationales for social work's moral mission, and of public versus private morality. These reflections are offered in the expectation that fuller analysis and further attempts at answers will follow, in this book and in other forums.

Social Work, Therapy, and Private Practice

As a general task, "Social work as a profession needs to regain its moral vision and idealism and even the moral passion that the old-time social workers had."[34] This calls for clarity about the nature of social work functions in helping people with problems of social dependency and deviant behavior. Social workers need to know clearly that they are agents of the community, with contractual obligations to represent the poor and disadvantaged, yet serving and mediating the interests of both poor and non-poor, the conforming and the deviant. Social workers are also obligated to foster social integration for all, to see that the social welfare system serves all needy members of the community. Facilitating and serving to balance the social forces for stability and change requires a just, fair judgment. This also means that social workers have an ethical responsibility to decide whether their own rule-bending or deviance, or their support of the deviance of others, is accountably beneficial and constructive, for themselves, their clients, and their communities.

Attaining clarity about social work functions involves discarding or revising the medical, mental health, psychotherapeutic model of social work services. From a social work point of view, helping to resolve problems of social functioning should explicitly require holistic attention to people, their life situations, and the moral/ethical issues involved. This requires, along with diagnosis and treatment, systemic assessment and intervention to facilitate needed changes in people and in social

institutions, for their complementary relationships and trans-
actions.

The current propensity of social workers to provide therapy
in private practice settings is troublesome. So is the pressure of
governmental policies on social agencies and on social workers
to engage in entrepreneurial funding arrangements for therapeutic services, and to be certified as mental health service providers. The acceptance of the medical, mental health model results
in the continued treatment of social workers as medical sub-
professionals, with restrictions on professional autonomy and
restraints on social work service provisions. There are even
graver negative results from the DSM III: It is mandated in
medical service and insurance contracts, though its use encourages subterfuge and malpractice.[35] More important is the encouragement of privatization of social services, which appears
to retreat from obligations of social action, community organization, and social institutional change.[36]

The medical-psychiatric paradigm for social work therapy
will decline when it is perceived as discrepant with social work
functions and value systems, and as having serious negative
consequences for the profession. It is inappropriate because
social work therapy is unlike other psychotherapeutic approaches. Social work has a distinctive focus on explicit values
and on social functioning of people, along with an ecological
systems perspective, and a repertoire of powerful situational
interventions. These features of social work practice enable
practitioners to better effect changes in persons and situations
and to achieve to some degree a just, caring relationship between the two.

The private practice of therapy is an area of social service,
however, for which there is much demand and reward, at a time
when there are severe financial constraints on social agencies.
Such private practice can be employed by the profession to
support societal task obligations, as in mandatory *pro bono*
work with social agencies.

There is some question about whether and how the mental
health model can be discarded, in view of this country's public
preoccupation with what are defined as matters of health and
mental health. Social workers have an opportunity as "mental
health" practitioners, to redefine "mental disorders" more ac-

curately as reactions to problems of social living and social dysfunction, so that these problems can be open to appropriate social work and other related, non-medical, perspectives and procedures.

Even though social work therapy is still conceptualized in terms of a medical, mental health paradigm, it does in part express the new moral orientation. The distinctive features of social work therapy emphasize moral/ethical objectives. The social work value of social justice is now seen as realized in the provision of social work therapy, including in private practice.[37]

The present emphasis on therapy can be considered a necessary stage in social work development, in keeping with the cyclical pattern of alternating focus on individual and on social reform. One can be confident that this pattern will continue. The very valuable knowledge and skills learned during the prior era of social activism are now being assimilated into repertoires of situational interventions. Social workers use these skills not only in therapeutic work, but also in work with community organizations and bureaucracies, and in social action activities through professional organizations. In addition, social workers are advancing their skills in providing more effective personal/ therapeutic services to individuals, families, and groups.

Also, clinical social workers are rediscovering, with new insights, that helping individuals and families from within a systems framework calls for systemic changes, which in many cases can be assured only by social worker situational intervention.[38] This means recognizing again that a good, supportive, resource-providing society is necessary for the generalization and maintenance of therapeutic achievements. Such a realization calls for renewed direct struggle for social reform, hopefully in more realistic ways than in the past, especially in the face of the collapse of Communist regimes in Europe. This process should be facilitated and reinforced, so that the next social reform era can find social workers better prepared to maximize the potential for further progress.

Morality and Ethics for Practice and Practitioners

Another important task concerns the basic moral nature of social work functions. The moral aspect should be made explicit, in ways that avoid connotations of judgmental, paternalistic attitudes. Social work philosophy and its moral/ethical theory need much more development to provide a credible, strong support for social work's moral mission and effective implementation. The fundamental social work values and concepts—e.g., of virtue and the social good—merit reaffirmation. The current concern with individual moral advancement calls for clarifying the ways in which individual self-realization and spiritual growth can be achieved through social interaction, reciprocal social relationships, and supportive, nurturing social resource systems. Significant gains have been made in recent years in developing practice theory, principles, and procedures to help clients and practitioners with moral/ethical dilemmas.[39] But much more of such work needs to be done.

Serving consciously as moral agents of the community and of the social welfare institution is an awesome responsibility. Fulfilling such responsibilities means balancing the forces for social change and social stability with regard for procedural justice and fairness. It includes, for example, serving as rule-changers and rule-enforcers, normative role models and social reformers, consolers and challengers, therapists and supervisors, certifiers for good or bad social identities.

A moral agent must care for, protect, and advocate for the dependent, orphaned, and rejected, the victims and casualties of a capitalist social economy. It also involves helping people refrain from destructive behavior; when destructive behavior does occur, it means helping people deal constructively with its consequences.

A particularly difficult responsibility is to serve *in parens patriae*, as caretakers for children, the aged, or other people demonstrably unable to care for themselves or for their own interests. This may involve decisions about removing children from abusive parents, or institutionalizing incompetent aged persons. Here is a thorny issue—how to carry out a necessary function, yet avoid the potential for being negatively paternalistic.[40]

On a Religious Rationale for Social Work Morality

The religious renewal of our times has intensified questions about how the social work practitioner can comfortably enact the moral agent role with or without a religious sanction, even with a contractual legal authority granted through legal licensing of social workers by the community. A major issue concerns whether and how a valid rationale for good behavior can be constructed on a nonreligious basis. A number of great thinkers, including Nietzsche and Marx, stood against religiously-based morality. Nontheistic humanists argue for a morality without a religious rationale, justifying moral/ethical behavior on the basis of evident human need and the requirements of a community of people living together in mutually beneficial ways.[41] There is a deeply-ingrained, traditional point of view that maintains the necessity of a religious basis for morality. Recently Glenn Tinder argued that we cannot be good without God, since human worth and dignity are God-given, and religious beliefs support responsible hope, faith, and action to help realize the just society that would be "the Kingdom of God."[42]

A relevant question here concerns the conception of religion and the nature of God that people formulate for themselves. Most people believe in God; they have very varied religious beliefs, including about the identity of God. There is a basic human need for spiritual consciousness, faith, and experience. A proper distinction must be observed between spirituality and religion, though many people identify spiritual with religious concepts and even misidentify spirituality with fundamentalist religious beliefs.[43] Joseph Campbell declared that the kingdom of God is within the person; "the God image is a metaphor for a spiritual experience."[44] He stated that, "Ethics and religion are not the same. . . . Ethics has to do with social values and religion has to do with personal, inward realization. . . . living in a society defines your realization of the inward values through the ethics of society."[45]

Whatever the merits in this controversy, we need to accept that there are, and will continue to be, social workers who are religious in both theistic and nontheistic terms, as well as those who are nonreligious and even anti-religious. We need moral theories and rationales that are credible and useful to all social workers. We also need to accept that each group has rationales for morality which they consider credible, and to respect their right to their opinions. Yet there is a basic set of values that needs to be recognized within this diversity. The important consideration is for moral theories that will enable social workers as members of a secular profession to understand the spiritual as well as religious needs of people, and to help people with their moral/ethical problems.

On Public and Private Morality

Another increasingly important question concerns the dividing line between public and private morality, for conduct in public and private life. Much deviant behavior is rationalized today on the grounds that private behavior of rational, consenting adults deserves much greater tolerance by the community. The domain of private conduct is thus held to be an area of individual autonomous action and self-fulfillment. Even granting the validity of this questionable assumption, the dividing line between private and public is often ambiguous, as are the appropriate moral standards for each sphere.

There is much current controversy, for example, about whether political representatives can be required by religious authorities or secular interests to oppose abortion or public funding of religious education, even in opposition to the popular will. How much right does the public have to knowledge about the private sexual lives of legislators? Under what conditions? What is acceptable intrusiveness about private financial, sexual, and other personal and family matters? Should these ever be open to governmental and public scrutiny?

The moral/ethical philosophical issue here is of major importance in clarifying the moral mission of social work. The social worker is charged with reconciling private moral/ethical beliefs and conduct with public judgments, decisions, and conduct, when these are in conflict. Most therapists learn to accept an abusive client or a murderous parent, distinguishing between the person and the behavior. For a social agency administrator, ethical questions about responsibilities, obligations, rights, caring, and justice contend with personal beliefs in regard to setting priorities and allocating resources for particular programs and types of clients. Ethical integrity and authenticity mean establishing congruency between public, professional, and private aspects of a social worker's life.

The ethical dilemmas about public and private morality are the subject of opposing philosophical views. There are universalists who believe in a universal ethical system for public and private conduct, and pluralists who accept the validity of diverse cultures, with relative values and moral codes. Those who believe that each person is the best judge of his or her own best interests favor large domains of private morality, whereas those who believe in human propensity for evil and destructiveness believe in a wide domain of public scrutiny, regulation, and protection. Private abuse of a child is culturally proscribed, but there is a controversy about whether spanking a child constitutes abuse.

Tinder declares that the current separation between the secular political and the religious spiritual is destructive and that the spiritual is inherently political, in one's relationships as a citizen and in civic affairs.[46] He states that union of the spiritual and the political is needed to actualize a democratic and just political community that respects the inherent worth and dignity of human beings.

In contrast, Stuart Hampshire affirms the human need for cultural and value pluralism, with different concepts of good, yet with a recognition of universal human needs and a common base of decency and justice that would protect against evil.[47] Such a minimum of decent fairness and rational procedural justice, he believes, would mediate the perpetual rivalries and conflicts within and between human beings and find "sufficient compromises to prevent madness in the soul and civil war or war between peoples." Because this is of major relevance for social work moral theory and helping process, the issue of distinctions between private and public morality needs our effort at resolution for practical purposes.

Conclusions

By their very nature, social workers are morally and politically liberal, believing in the inherent goodness and perfectibility of all human beings. This belief is associated with the moral mission of the profession, and of its role as a moral agent in the societal processes of social change and social stability. But the reality is that social workers seek the good in imperfect people and an imperfect society. The vast majority of social work clients and the major subject of social work ministrations involve sins and evils—hatred, murder, greed, sloth, infidelity, and exploitation—conduct which today we politely call dependency, deviant behavior, or even mental illness. These realities of social work practice are hard to reconcile with basic beliefs in the inherent goodness of people when one is at the battlefront of direct social services in urban ghettos.

Current shifts in public morality present difficult contradictions and a great deal of confusion about right and wrong. There is a public adoption of conservative attitudes and higher standards of personal conduct and interpersonal relationships, yet there continues to be a high incidence of destructive behavior, in terms of interpersonal violence, drug addiction, and sexually-transmitted disease epidemics. Many social workers are similarly conflicted about moral standards and choices. Because they have a particularly important assignment—to help people with moral dilemmas—social workers have a special opportunity to help resolve these dilemmas for society and for themselves. Taking on the challenges of the tasks and the issues identified in this chapter should enable social workers to renew their crucial moral mission in helping people lead good lives in a good society.

Notes

1. Among many histories of social work that detail this religious institutional background, see: James Leiby, *History of Social Welfare and Social Work in the United States* (New York: Columbia University Press, 1978). Charles S. Loch, *Three Thousand Years of Social Service* (London: Macmillan, 1910). Reinhold Niebuhr, *The Contribution of Religion to Social Work* (New York: Columbia University Press, 1932). Stuart A. Queen, *Social Work in the Light of History* (Philadelphia: Lippincott, 1922). Max Siporin, "Contribution of Religious Values to Social Work and the Law," *Social Thought* 12 (1986) 4:35–50. Frank D. Watson, *The Charity Organization Movement in the United States* (New York: Macmillan, 1922).

2. Edward T. Devine, *The Practice of Charity: Individual, Associated and Organized* (New York: Lentilhon and Co., 1901). The quota-

tions that follow are on pp. 10 and 155. Around the turn of the century, Devine was the director of the Charity Organization Society of New York City, and also served as director of the New York School of Social Work.

3. Charles S. Loch, *A Great Ideal and Its Champion* (London: Allen & Unwin, 1923), 23. Loch was the director of the London, England, Charity Organization Society from 1875 to 1913.

4. James Leiby, "The Moral Foundations of Social Welfare and Social Work: A Historical Review," *Social Work* 30 (July/August 1985): 323–30. The subject of the C.O.S. was studied as part of the new science of sociology in Charles R. Henderson, *An Introduction to the Study of the Dependent, Defective and Delinquent Classes* (Boston: D.C. Heath, 1893).

5. On "the prevention of crime and pauperism" as the primary purpose of early social work, see Frank D. Watson, *The Charity Organization Movement in the United States* (New York: Macmillan, 1922), 53.

6. The social worker leadership in this cultural shift is well described by Robert H. Bremner, *From the Depths* (New York: New York University Press, 1956).

7. James O.S. Huntington, "Philanthropy and Morality," in Jane Addams et al., *Philanthropy and Social Progress*, (New York: Crowell) 157–204.

8. Joseph Tuckerman, "Introduction," in Baron Joseph Marie DeGerando, *The Visitor of the Poor* (Boston: Hilliard, Grey, Little & Wilkins, 1832), i–xxx.

9. Charles S. Levy, "Values and Ethics: Foundation of Social Work," in Sidney Dillick, ed., *Value Foundations of Social Work* (Detroit: School of Social Work, Wayne State University, 1984), 20.

10. Robert deForest, "Justice, Not Charity," *Charities* 7, 23 November 1901):431.

11. Edward T. Devine, *The Principles of Relief* (New York: Macmillan, 1904), 6. It is of interest that on p. 7, he spoke of "the professional service . . . of social work."

12. For an exposition of these societal task functions, see Max Siporin, *Introduction to Social Work Practice* (New York: Macmillan, 1975), 32–47.

13. On this social control and social change mediating function, see Brian J. Heraud, *Sociology and Social Work* (Oxford: Pergamon Press, 1970), 143–218. Max Siporin, "Deviant Behavior Theory in Social Work Diagnosis and Treatment," *Social Work* 10 (May 1965):59–67; idem, "Deviance, Morality and Social Work Therapy," *Social Thought* 11 (1985) 4:11–24.

14. For fuller discussions of the moral philosophy, nature and mission of social work by this author, see Siporin, *Introduction to Social Work Practice*, 61–98; idem, "Moral Philosophy in Social Work Today," *Social Service Review* 56 (1982) 516–38; idem, Morality and Immorality in Working with Clients," *Social Thought* 9 (1983) 4:10–28; idem, "The Social Work Ethic," *Social Thought* 15 (1989) 3/4:42–52. See also, Felix Biestek, *The Casework Relationship* (Chicago: Loyola University Press, 1957). Frederic G. Reamer, *Ethical Dilemmas in Social Service*, 2nd ed. (New York: Columbia University Press, 1990). M. Vincentia Joseph, ed., *Ethics—Social Thought* 15 (1989) 3/4:1–148. Noel Timms, *Social Work Values: An Inquiry* (London: Routledge & Kegan Paul, 1983). Noel Timms and David Watson, eds., *Philosophy in Social Work* (London: Routledge & Kegan Paul, 1978). Ann Weick, "Reconceptualizing the Philosophic Perspective of Social Work," *Social Service Review* 61 (1987):218–30.

15. John J. Hughes, "Toward a Moral Philosophy for Social Work," *Social Thought* 10 (1984) 2:3–17.

16. For a helpful explanation of the rationale for social work moral/ethical philosophy as based on our understanding of a person's essential sociality and social relations, see Robert T. Constable, "Relations and Membership: Foundations for Ethical Thinking in Social Work," in Joseph, ed., *Ethics*, 53–66. For a recent discussion of social work moral theory, see Robert W. Imre, "Moral Theory for Social Work," *Social Thought* 15 (1989):18–27.

17. The yoking of charity and justice was well discussed by Stephen S. Wise, "Charity versus Justice," in Alexander Johnson, ed., *Proceedings, National Conference on Charities and Correction* (Fort Wayne, Ind.: Press of the Fort Wayne Printing Co., 1909), 26–28. Jane Addams, "Charity and Social Justice," *Proceedings, National Conference of Charities and Correction* (Fort Wayne, Ind: Press of the Fort Wayne Printing Co., 1910), 2–3. Charles Frankel, *Some Paradoxes in the Ideal of Welfare* (New Orleans, La.: School of Social Work, Tulane University, 1965). For a fuller discussion of these both/and sets of values, see: Siporin, *Introduction to Social Work Practice*, 73–74. It is of interest that many social work practitioners, particularly women social workers, combine justice and caring moral orientations in making ethical practice judgments, according to a study by Arthur Dobrin, "Ethical Judgments of Male and Female Social Workers," *Social Work* 34 (1989):451–55.

18. "Code of Ethics of the National Association of Social Workers," *Encyclopedia of Social Work*, 18th ed. (Silver Spring, Md.: NASW, 1987) 951–56.

19. For example: M. Vincentia Joseph, "A Model for Ethical Deci-

sion Making in Clinical Practice," in Carel B. Germain, ed., *Advances in Clinical Practice* (Silver Spring, Md.: NASW, 1985), 201–217. Harold Lewis, "Ethical Assessment," *Social Casework* 65 (1984): 203–211. Charles S. Levy, *Social Work Ethics* (New York: Human Sciences Press, 1976). Frank Lowenberg and Ralph Dolgoff, *Ethical Decisions for Social Work Practice*, 2nd ed. (Itasca, Ill.: Peacock Publishers, 1985). Reamer, *Ethical Dilemmas*. Margaret L. Rhodes, *Ethical Dilemmas in Social Work Practice* (Boston: Routledge & Kegan Paul, 1986).

20. Frederick G. Reamer, "Values and Ethics," in *Encyclopedia of Social Work* (note 18), pp. 801–9.

21. Ann A. Abbott, *Professional Choices: Values at Work* (Silver Spring, Md: National Association of Social Workers, 1988); the quotations in the next sentence appear on p. 112. Further support for these conclusions is given in Linda Cherrey Reeser and Irwin Epstein, *Professionalism and Activism in Social Work: The Sixties, the Eighties, and the Future* (New York: Columbia University Press, 1990) and David Wagner, *The Quest for a Radical Profession* (Lanham, Md.: University Press of America, 1990).

22. On these individualistic and currently conservative trends, see: Robert N. Bellah et al., *Habits of the Heart* (New York: Harper & Row, 1985). Allan Bloom, *The Closing of the American Mind* (New York: Simon & Schuster, 1987).

23. Richard H. Price and Sallie S. Smith, "Two Decades of Reform in the Mental Health System," in Edward Seidman, ed., *Handbook of Social Intervention* (Beverly Hills, Calif.: Sage Publications, 1983), 408–437. E. Fuller Torrey, *Nowhere to Go: The Tragic Odyssey of the Homeless Mentally Ill*, 2nd ed. (New York: Aldine Publishing Co., 1984).

24. On the mental health ideology, see: Peter Conrad and Joseph W. Schneider, *Deviance and Medicalization: From Badness to Sickness*, (St. Louis, Mo: Mosby, 1980); Thomas Szasz, *The Myth of Psychotherapy*, (New York: Anchor Books, 1979). Thomas J. Scheff, *Being Mentally Ill*, 2nd ed. (New York: Aldine Publishing Co., 1984).

25. Mary E. Richmond, *The Long View*, ed. Joanna C. Colcord and Ruth Z. Mann (New York: Russell Sage Foundation, 1930), 584–92.

26. A critical evaluation of the consequences of these historical controversies is still to be done. On some of the negative consequences of the social activism of the 1960s, see: William Schwartz, "Private Troubles and Public Issues: One Social Work Job or Two?" in *Proceedings, National Conference of Social Work, 1969* (New York: Columbia University Press, 1969), 22–43. For a positive view, see Wagner, *The Quest*, especially p. 211.

27. For example: Howard Goldstein, "The Neglected Moral Link

in Social Work Practice," *Social Work* 32 (May/June 1987):181–86. Thomas P. Holland, "Values, Faith and Professional Practice," *Social Thought* 15 (1989) 2:28–40. Harold Lewis, "Ethics and the Private Non-Profit Human Service Organization," *Administration in Social Work* 13 (1989) 2:1–14. See also the works of Siporin in note 14, above.

28. Max Siporin, "Have You Heard the One about Social Work Humor?," *Social Casework* 65 (1984):459–64. Describes some of the negative as well as positive images of social work characters in recent novels.

29. James A. Jones and Abraham Alcabes, "Clients Don't Sue: The Invulnerable Social Worker," *Social Casework* 70 (1989):414–20.

30. See note 21 above.

31. Edward R. Canda, "Spirituality, Religious Diversity and Social Work Practice," *Social Casework* 69 (1988):238–47. Robert T. Constable, "Values, Religion, and Social Work Practice," *Social Thought* 4 (1983) 2:28–41. Catherine Faver, "Religion, Research and Social Work," *Social Thought* 12 (1986) 3:19–29. Eleanor H. Judah, "A Spirituality of Professional Service," *Social Thought* 11 (1985) 4:25–35. M. Vincentia Joseph, "The Religious and Spiritual Aspects of Clinical Practice," *Social Thought* 13 (1987) 1:12–23. See also note 32 below.

32. For example: David Brandon, *Zen in the Art of Helping* (London: Routledge & Kegan Paul, 1976). David G. Edwards, *Existential Psychotherapy* (New York: Gardner Press, 1982). Donald F. Krill, "Existential Social Work," in Francis J. Turner, ed., *Social Work Treatment*, 3rd ed. (New York: The Free Press, 1986), 181–218. From a philosophical perspective, the functionalist school is part of the existentialist approach; for an exposition of this theoretical orientation, see Shankar A. Yelaja, "Functional Theory for Social Work Practice," in Turner, ed., *Social Work Treatment*, 46–67.

33. For example: Howard Goldstein, "A Cognitive-Humanistic Approach to Practice," in Howard Goldstein, ed., *Creative Change* (New York: Tavistock Publications, 1984), 3–66; Martha Heineman Pieper, "The Heuristic Paradigm," *Smith College Studies in Social Work* 60 (1989) 1:8–34. Edmund Sherman, "Hermeneutics, Human Science, and Social Work," *Social Thought* 13 (1987) 1:34–41. Francis J. Turner, ed., *Social Work Treatment* (New York: The Free Press, 1986) 91–129. Stanley L. Witkin, "Toward a Scientific Social Work," *Journal of Social Work Research* 12 (1989) 3/4:83–98.

34. Siporin, "Moral Philosophy."

35. Stuart Kirk, Max Siporin, and Herb Kutchins, "The Prognosis for Social Work Diagnosis," *Social Casework* 70 (1989):295–304.

36. Harold Lewis, "Ethics and the Private Nonprofit Human Service Organization," *Administration in Social Work* 13 (1989) 2:1–14.

37. Jerome C. Wakefield, "Psychotherapy, Distributive Justice, and Social Work," *Social Service Review* 62 (1988):187–210, 353–82.

38. This renewed problem-person situation or ecosystems emphasis is given, for example, in Carel B. Germain and Alex Gitterman, *The Life Model of Social Work Practice* (New York: Columbia University Press, 1980). Dean H. Hepworth and Jo Ann Larsen, *Direct Social Work Practice: Theory and Skills*, 3rd ed. (Homewood, Ill.: Dorsey Press, 1990). Curtis Jansen and Oliver Harris, *Family Treatment in Social Work Practice*, 2d ed. (Itasca, Ill.: F.E. Peacock Publishers, 1986).

39. See note 19 above.

40. Marcia Abramson, "Autonomy vs. Paternalistic Beneficience: Practice Strategies," *Social Casework* 70 (1989):101–105, idem, "The Autonomy-Paternalism Dilemma in Social Work Practice," *Social Casework* 66 (1985):387–93. Harlan Hahn, "Paternalism and Public Policy," *Society* 25 (1983):36–46. Frederic G. Reamer, "The Concept of Paternalism in Social Work," *Social Service Review* 57 (1983):254–71. Ruben Schindler, "Paternalism—The Jewish Dimension," *Journal of Jewish Communal Service* 64 (1987):311–16.

41. For example, the various articles on religion and ethics, in Paul Kurtz, ed., *Moral Problems in Contemporary Society*, (Englewood Cliffs, N.J.: Prentice-Hall, 1969), particularly the paper by Kai Nielsen, "Ethics Without Religion," 17–32. Paul Kurtz, *Forbidden Fruit: The Ethics of Humanism* (Buffalo, N.Y.: Prometheus Books, 1988).

42. Glenn Tinder, "Can We Be Good Without God?" *Atlantic Monthly* 264 (December 1989): 69–85.

43. On this kind of conceptual confusion, see the interchange of letters between Paul Sanzenbach, Edward Canda, and M. Vincentia Joseph in *Social Casework*, 70 (1989):571–75.

44. Joseph Campbell, *An Open Life*, ed. John M. Maher and Dennis Briggs, eds., (Burdett, N.Y.: Larson Publications, 1988), 87.

45. *Ibid.*, 86.

46. Tinder, "Can We Be Good?"

47. Stuart Hampshire, *Innocence and Experience* (Cambridge, Mass.: Harvard University Press, 1989). The quotation in the next sentence appears on p. 189.

CHAPTER SIX

The Moral Basis for a Radical Reconstruction of Social Work

James O. Billups

Introduction

In recent decades social work practitioners, academicians, and students have encountered somewhat foreign-sounding and radically oriented practice-relevant concepts. These concepts have encouraged interested social workers to adopt new ideas or, at least, old ideas thought of in new ways. Examples of such concepts are "anti-establishment action roles," "conscientization," "animation," "liberating praxis," "radical humanism," "radical structuralism," "client-led militancy," and "militant professionalism."[1] During this same period there have been several book-length elaborations and research reports describing and analyzing proposals for radical changes in the means and ends, if not also the system and substance, of social work practice and social work education.[2]

Prompting the emergence of concepts for a more radical social work practice has been dissatisfaction with conventional practice. Much present-day social work is characterized by what we can refer to as a disastrously split vision. Students and practitioners of the profession tend to pursue educational preparation and careers that point them either toward micro-oriented or macro-oriented practice, individual therapy or social reform, people helping or system-changing. The resulting bifurcation has, in the eyes of various critics, seriously diminished the scope and effectiveness of social work.[3]

The problem for the profession is not only the split vision and bifurcation, but the unevenly balanced distribution of practitioners and practitioner efforts. From the dichotomously paired options, most students and practitioners have chosen or have been otherwise recruited, steered, or assigned to the micro-oriented, individual therapy and people-helping arenas widely known as casework, direct treatment services, or clinical social work practice.[4] For individual practitioners and for social workers in the aggregate, this widely prevailing pattern of educational and career choice and assignment has had profound social, political, and moral consequences, at least in the United States, if not in other countries. One author has summarized the situation as follows:

> Although 'social work' refers to a whole range of activities, social workers are primarily trained as 'caseworkers' and the vast majority have been engaged in this sort of work since the beginning of the century ... [Accordingly,] social workers [have been] drawn well away from economics, labor relations, environmental factors, and especially political analyses. ... The concentration by the caseworker on the individual and his [or her] family makes the implicit assumption that society is fundamentally sound and that 'problems' lie only in the individual's inability to cope. Thus is the status quo conserved.[5]

If this is the practice pattern and outcome that continues to predominate in many parts of the world, then we can safely assume that social work deserves to be reconstructed. Whether or not such a reconstruction draws on many or few of the radically oriented practice concepts mentioned at the outset, it must depart in some fundamental ways from the prevailing system of practice. The endeavor is likely, therefore, to be sufficiently threatening to vested interests to be viewed by most social workers as radical. But we accept that to be so labeled is part of the professional tradition, in that "social work and social workers have, at different periods, described themselves or have been described by others in radical terms. . . ."[6]

Morality and Social Work

Morality, as we shall use it here, pertains to the conduct of human affairs and relationships between people at various levels of human systems, with consideration by the moral agents—in this case, social workers—for the effects of their motives and actions on the lives of others. The moral principles used for professional conduct obtain their justification, ideally at least, from the sacred, from impartial reasoning, and/or from concern for human welfare. At their most basic level, these principles are universal, potentially understood and respected by social workers everywhere. But there are multiple moral subcultures within the profession, and a reasonable moral consensus among social workers, while desirable, appears for now to be achievable only in the somewhat distant future.

On a historical note, there has been a shift of emphasis within the profession in the use of moral concepts and in the ways in which social workers think about morality. Whereas in the latter part of the nineteenth and early part of the twentieth century the interest of many pioneer social workers centered on the morality of clients and their moral rectitude, "the concern that emerged during the mid-years of the twentieth century began to lean toward the morality and ethics . . . of social work and its practitioners."[7]

In one form or another, the observation articulated by Lindeman became an increasingly frequent theme. He wrote, "what takes place between the social worker and the citizen constitutes a moral equation."[8] More recent authors have reached much the same conclusion.[9] In colorful language, "The politics of social work involves not only the moral crusades of policy reform, but also the day-to-day moral hustle of the social worker's professional life."[10] Thus, there is every reason to suggest that moral political issues are the very guts of social work practices."[11]

Although there seems to be little question that a moral dimension of practice has been and continues to be an integral part of social work, there is considerable question as to what is meant by the concept. It comes as no surprise that for most members of the profession, just as for the general public and even for philosophers, "moral" remains "a very slippery term indeed."[12] However, due to the relatively recent work on moral theory within the profession, the term and the concept need not be quite so elusive as before. For example, Hughes has explicated criteria for an ideal moral framework and concluded that among the various options, the classic humanist theory of natural law holds the most promise for social work. He has maintained,

> The common moral ground on which social workers could easily stand together is that of the natural virtues: prudence, justice, courage, temperance, respect for knowledge and truth, generosity, self-discipline and tolerance . . . whether they call them virtues or not. Indeed, it seems fair to say that such virtues represent the very essence of the individual and collective humanity we [social workers] idealize.[13]

With a view to much this same sort of idealized dual concern for individual and collective humanity, Siporin has advanced a concept of the moral dimension of social work to be applied within a multilevel, ecosystemic perspective. He has urged not only that social workers themselves serve as moral agents, but also that they learn to influence individuals and families, supportive networks, and larger social institutional structures of society to become morally concerned and responsible entities as well.[14]

Also, Lewis has formulated practice presuppositions and principles that are considered, irrespective of the practice concentration of the social worker, to be universally applicable in working relationships with disadvantaged and vulnerable people. These presuppositions-principles appear to illustrate the moral obligation of practitioners to make assessments and interventions from a holistic, humanitarian, and democratic, if not also an egalitarian practice perspective. Like Hughes and Siporin, Lewis conveys a respect and active concern for both individual and collective humanity. Two of his practice principles are, "Institutionalized restrictions which limit opportunities, as well as the personal shortcomings of the client which may curtail . . . options, are legitimate targets for change . . . "; and, "opportunities to participate in the development of programs, in the formulation of policies and procedures, as well as in the practice decisions directly affecting their lives, must be afforded the disadvantaged as a minimum expectation of organizations and practices intended to help them."[15]

While it is still true that social workers care for the poor and disadvantaged and are committed to social justice and equality in democratic and mutually responsible social relations, Siporin finds that social workers in recent years have entered into a period of fragmented and weakened moral vision. He adds that a libertarian social work morality has become the more prevalent and controversial of the various moral subcultures within the profession. This libertarian morality translates into an egoistic and individualistic ethic based on an overall moral relativism that supports the development of narcissistic personalities and a psychologism that focuses on inner psychic forces, rather than on broader psychosocial explanations of human behavior with which social workers have been traditionally identified.[16]

The focus of much social work practice is centered on the personal preoccupations of people and the fostering of their self-fulfillment, with little regard for others except those persons in their most immediate environment. The excessive emphasis on individualism in American society has been too uncritically accepted by many social workers, without sufficient attention given to how individuals' decisions and actions regarding their own self-realization affect others. Katz has argued,

> The trend toward narcissism, if not checked, may well rob succeeding generations of the critical dimension of social concern. . . . Social work practice . . . has a significant role to play in helping restore the understanding that the . . . goal is a life in which many people count and in which life is judged not only on personal fulfillment, but also on how one has helped others toward that same goal.[17]

Clearly, a relativistic and individualistic moral ethic at work both in American society and in social work stands in sharp contrast to the moral presuppositions and principles that point social workers toward the interrelated goals of enhancing both individual potential and collective human realization. As Siporin has warned, "There is an increasingly evident contradiction between this individualistic, 'self fulfillment' orientation expressed by many social workers and the humanistic values of equality, democracy, justice, altruism, social responsibility, and mutual aid, which are publicly and ritually professed by the social work profession."[18]

Relativistic, libertarian morality puts at risk the advancement of efforts at developing consensus on a socially conscious morality as a basis for a philosophy of social work; at the same time, it endangers efforts at developing a unified and generic core of social work practice, and thereby threatens continuation of the profession itself. As Leighninger has noted, "without common bases of philosophy and practice, professions can lose their cohesion and distinctiveness, relinquishing functions to other professions and even dividing into smaller constituent parts."[19]

A Reconstruction (or Reinvigoration): Four Major Steps

One of the principal steps toward helping stem the tide of a weakened moral vision on one hand and an increased practice divergence on the other is for practitioners, educators, and students to make a broad-scale return to the historically grounded social work's simultaneous dual focus on and concern for both sides of the person-environment complex. Social work focus during the past century has oscillated between the personal/emotional and the social/political aspects of life; yet the profession has refrained from giving itself completely to one or the other—either to helping people only with their personal troubles or to helping larger social units only with public issues. Even though a well-balanced professional attention to both sides of the person-environment equation has seldom if ever been widely achieved, nonetheless an obligation of the profession to balance its efforts more equally has been strongly urged for some time. As one writer has put it,

> Suffering humanity in the mass and the individual caught up in the suffering with his [or her] own unique problems—these are two sides of the same coin. . . . From Jane Addams through Mary Richmond through Edith Abbott through Charlotte Towle, and through many other leaders here [in the United States] and in other countries, the dual obligation of the profession to bring about social reform and to help the individual and family has been of constant concern.[20]

The reconstruction or reinvigoration of social work proposed herein requires the creative inclusiveness of the simultaneous dual focus on aiding people and improving their social institutions. This is not only an obligation of the profession as a whole (and here is where we become a bit radical), but of its individual practitioners as well, no matter their personal predilections or professional specializations. As Pumphrey observed some years ago, and others since have at least partially agreed, "the answer to the long search for the unique characteristics of social work might be found in a feeling of obligation *always* to consider social needs when dealing with individuals, and the effect on individuals when dealing with groups or communities."[21] If the profession and its members were to adopt this practice principle as a moral imperative, it would go far in making social work a much less fragmented response and a more coherent and unified force in societies around the world.

A second fundamental step toward reconstructing or strengthening social work's moral base is to identify (or reidentify) with the ultimate value and principle goal of social work. One social work theorist, William Gordon, put forth this proposed wording for the ultimate professional value, eloquent in its simplicity despite its comprehensiveness, and for its faith in individual persons and in collective humanity: "It is good and desirable for . . . [people] to fulfill [their] potential, to realize . . . [themselves] and to balance this with essentially equal effort to help others fulfill their capacities and realize themselves."[22] In an individualistic, atomized, highly competitive urban society such as the United States, this proposed emphasis on development of human potentialities for one and all through cooperative efforts has its own sort of radical ring to it.

But Gordon did not stop there. He expressed the need for the profession and its members to establish values and set goals that transcend the here and now, and include not only breadth but temporal length. He maintained that a central value theme in the profession, still dormant and waiting to be unleashed, is that of human realization—"the continued growth and unfolding of one's potential in the direction of his [or her] own choosing and in ways that facilitate the realization of others over the lifetime of the individual . . . and over the generations."[23] He added that while this perspective ". . . retains the clear view of each individual, there is nothing to preclude its being generalized to any number of individuals comprising families, groups, neighborhoods, or communities. ... In other words, the unit of perspective remains the individual without, however, imposing any requirements on the mode and point of intervention."[24]

Other work by Gordon poses not only the ultimate value and goal of social work, but also the key concepts that he maintains must be developed and used in conjunction with one another if social work is to formulate integrative and generative ideas, in order to grow and develop as a profession and to make its own distinctive, much-needed contribution to humankind. He writes about what can be considered a third step in reconstructing social work, the identification of key generic concepts.

> The ultimate value and goal of social work—what it most of all wants for people—is the fullest possible realization of the *human potential* in them. This goal, of course, is shared with many others, but social work's particular strength, expertise, or professional competence, and ultimately its science, lies in so *matching* up the *coping capabilities* of people with their *impinging environments* that the resulting *transactions* contribute maximally both to the development of their *human potential* and to an environment conducive to that *development in others*.[25]

To elaborate briefly: Social workers drawn to and motivated by the simultaneous dual focus and concern, the ultimate value and goal, as well as the associated key concepts outlined and emphasized above, will tend to place great importance on facilitating reciprocal, mutually supportive, and growth-inducing human relationships. One recent proponent of a social work so conceived has extended these central ideas in order to further clarify the scope and nature of an imaginatively inclusive social work:

> We value and therefore promote synergistic social systems in all our activities. Synergistic social systems are families, small groups, organizations and communities that function simultaneously for the good of both the individual and the system.

These values require that all social workers possess fundamental knowledge of the potential for and obstacles to synergistic social interactions as well as the process, methods and skills to enable such interactions. This . . . includes the theory, principles and skills for assessing mismatches, mediating to enable matches, and evaluating the degree of synergy that results from . . . practice.[26]

This brings us to a final step in reconstructing, or at least reinvigorating, social work practice. This step calls for educating and expecting social workers to broaden their repertoires of interventive approaches and techniques consistent with the simultaneous dual focus and concern, the ultimate value and goal, as well as Gordon's key concepts. This critical step requires turning professional attention in concerted ways to at least three recently emergent (if not also convergent) practice approaches that are in essential support of the integrative and generative ideas already set forth.

The first of the three practice approaches is that of the generalist. This approach is widely acknowledged to be closely associated with broad-ranging people-environment assessments and with interventions in individuals, families, groups, and communities.[27] The generalist-oriented social work practitioner engages in "thinking past the particular situation to implications at a broader level" and also "considers the possibility of interventions on different levels simultaneously."[28] Goldstein points out that this approach to practice has other far-reaching potential influences beyond the effects it may have on the practice of individual social workers. He states, "Generalism confronts the profession with a radical alternative to its current operating philosophy, its role within the fractionalized service delivery system, and its educational programs. . . . It offers a thoughtful and definitive means of attacking the conditions of living and problems of practice."[29]

The feminist approach to social work practice is highly compatible with the generalist approach. It holds perhaps equal potential for facilitating radical change in both the profession and its practice. Especially valuable is the feminist ideology based in part on such premises as the "ability to see unity and connectedness in seemingly disparate events" and the "importance of elimination of false dichotomies and artificial separa-

tions." Operationalized, such organizing ideas help practitioners see that "the personal is political" and, thus, that there
is need for social workers to break out of counselor-only roles
and to serve also as activists.[30] "The interconnection between
individual and social existence is a cornerstone of feminism
in theory and in practice," according to Morell; "simply put,
feminism . . . seeks individual liberation through collective activity, embracing both personal and social change."[31]

Social development is the third highly compatible and convergent practice approach. It is consistent with a broadly based
people-environment transactional construct that is also central
to the generalist and feminist approaches. Social development
is conceived of as an intersystemic, integrated approach designed to facilitate developing the capacity of people to work
continuously for their own welfare, and developing a society's
institutions so that human needs are met at all levels.[32] According to Spergel, "The basic perspective of social development, on the American scene and in other countries, assumes
. . . social work . . . should look closely and explicitly at various
interrelated aspects of the social environment and [hu]-
man[kind], and intervene in more systematic fashion."[33] By
such a conception, the social development approach encompasses various professional tasks, including community build-
ing as well as individual intervention.[34] Moreover, much like
the other two approaches, the social development approach
has its potential for far-reaching effects. It calls for increasing
numbers of social workers to assume a much enlarged and
changed domain of interest and commitment. In Sanders'
words,

> If the social work profession is to be responsive to the new
> areas of . . . concern such as . . . humanizing [individual and
> social] development, we are faced with the task of radically
> restructuring education and practice. . . . In addition to the
> traditional service emphasis, there is the vital need for . . .
> focusing on issues of . . . institutional and policy change, re-
> spect for diverse people and cultural traditions and concerns
> related to overall quality of life.[35]

All three of these relatively recent conceptions of social
work practice approaches have emerged primarily since the

"revolutionary sixties," and their proponents have shown considerable agreement in what they have framed as the focus, value base and purpose, and key organizing concepts that are considered to be the responsibility of social work and of social workers. Consistent with the thinking represented in the previous discussion, Alexander has reported that there has been, at least on the intellectual level, ample recognition that "the professional's obligation is no longer weighted on the side of personal problem solving, clinical practice, and personality alteration or, conversely, on the side of social action, institutional modification, or environmental manipulation. Rather, it is focused on the points between people and their social institutions."[36] Moreover, as Alexander maintains, laudably but perhaps a bit too optimistically for now, "the profession is coming to understand that no social worker is thoroughly professional who ignores either side of the equation of life."[37]

Vested Interests and the Public Good

One problem for the profession in moving toward an imaginatively inclusive practice resides, however, with various vested interests that seem to oppose the kind of moral obligation and professional uniqueness that Alexander, Pumphrey, Gordon, and others have proposed. The profession and its members need to wrestle vigorously and overcome, or at least neutralize, the intransigence of three oppositional forces. For one, Goldstein points to the entrenched, pragmatic orientation of categorical and independent service programs in the social service delivery system as a major obstacle to a more holistic thinking and practice. Such programs and systems, he relates,

> because of their myopic and exclusive perceptions, . . . often fail to respond to the multifaceted problems of living. . . . All agencies and institutions become, over time, self maintaining systems, vested interests, or, in the vernacular, 'private turfs.' . . . This being the case, an established agency will be unwilling . . . to merge, cooperate or move towards a unified approach to service delivery.[38]

Then, too, professional education tends to perpetuate a categorical model, thereby providing another principal obstacle to

development of a more inclusive social work practice. Again,
Goldstein notes,

> On a fundamental level, the educational process is not
> entirely sympathetic to a holistic . . . orientation. Education
> generally tends to fractionalize knowledge in the form
> of disciplines, fields, specializations, concentrations, and
> courses. . . . The catch is that educators give little credence
> to this weakness and assume a pragmatic posture to justify
> specialization in education . . . one can . . . surmise that educa-
> tional programs, much like other entrenched establishments,
> tend to resist modification.[39]

Still another type of vested interest is the growing private,
proprietary, and autonomous practice, essentially consisting of
"popular psychotherapy" of "individual repair," which today
in the United States is engaged in on at least a part-time basis
by up to 25 percent of the members of the National Association
of Social Workers.[40] This vested interest poses serious concerns.
According to Schwartz, this type of practice can often operate
from "a simplistic and erroneous over-identification of ends
and means; that is, inasmuch as the end of social work is to
benefit individuals, then the best means of accomplishing this
is usually to treat the individual directly."[41] This, however,
often "leads to the illusion that if all member clients or patients
can be treated, one by one, or in small groups, the social problems of which they may be victims will then disappear."[42]

A more inclusive view of the social phenomena of concern
to social work would embrace practice not with individuals
only (or even with individuals and their most immediate or
proximal environments), but with much larger social units as
well. To do so, Reamer urges elsewhere in this volume that
social workers assume an enlightened and expanded view of
the public good that reflects concern not only for individual
clients, but also for "the general citizenry, . . . especially the
most vulnerable and least advantaged."[43] He worries, however,
that the rush toward private, proprietary, and autonomous social work practice in the United States is "accompanied by
significant financial (and perhaps status-sensitive) incentives
to cater to more rather than less affluent clients. . . . Thus,

rather than pursuing the public good in an enlightened fashion, the public may be served by a significant number of practitioners . . . pursuing 'enlightened self-interest.' "[44] Basically, then, a moral dilemma for social workers in an increasingly privatized market economy centers on whether to continue pursuing a narrower view of the public good focused principally on work with the personal needs of individuals (especially the needs of individuals of middle and higher socioeconomic status who can pay with cash or through insurance coverage), or to move toward solidifying a broader communal view of the public good that includes practice directed at improving conditions of the masses of people as well. I, like many other authors already cited, think that the moral imperative of social workers is to view the public good in a broader rather than narrower fashion and, accordingly, to engage in social work practice that is more inclusive rather than more exclusive.

Quiet or Loud Radicalism?

The remaining question concerns how radically and by which means the profession and its members need to move in the direction of promoting the broader public good.

Given the above-mentioned strongly entrenched vested interests,[45] in order to become effectively identified with both sides of the equation of life, members of the profession will need to become engaged, at a minimum, in what one writer has referred to as the "quiet radicalism" of social work orthodoxy.[46] This kind of radicalism actually dates back to at least 1922 when Mary Richmond wrote that ". . . family caseworkers should be making social discoveries as a by-product of successful casework. They should be bearing faithful witness to the need for social reforms wherever their daily work reveals the need."[47] This quiet radicalism has more recently been constructed and identified as "the documenting model," wherein each person receiving direct social work services is viewed by the social worker not only as an individual, but simultaneously as a member of a larger population group of special concern, such as the unemployed, or dependent and neglected children. Thus, each direct contact by a professional social worker is both an opportunity for service and an opportunity to document the consequences of existing policies and programs in the lives of people. Under this model of social work, on some sort of regular basis,

> the practitioner makes (documents) an accounting to the sup-
> porting community not only of direct services rendered, but
> also of what he [or she] has learned ... about the present
> adequacy of program design, its feasibility and functional rela-
> tionship to articulated policy goals, and the adequacy and
> implications of existing problem conceptualizations ... [in
> order] to stimulate corrective community action.[48]

There is at least one other way of reconstructing or reinvigorating both one's understanding of social work practice and the
practices of the corporate whole of the profession. What we
shall refer to as "loud radicalism" is represented by a model of
social work practice somewhat more extensive than the documenting model. The proponents of this practice model, too,
find that "efforts to remediate individual and family problems
can[not] occur apart from broader efforts to restructure the institutional context from which these problems emerge;" moreover, they assert that "problems of the worker in defining the
nature, scope and direction of his/her work can[not] be dealt
with separately from attempts to enable clients to gain a similar
sense of control and definition of their environments."[49] These
authors maintain that a new integration of social treatment and
social action can be forthcoming with the help of concepts and
processes of "empowerment ... through the incorporation ...
of the Latin American concept of conscientization and the
French concept of animation."[50] In this radical/egalitarian view
of practice, each of these concepts and processes facilitates the
compelling need for clients and practitioners to engage together
in group processes whereby they examine "political-economic
issues, particularly those concerning resource deprivation, resource acquisition and utilization, and the consequent impact
of these realities on the relative powerlessness of clients and
[social] workers."[51] Critical reflection, revised perceptions of
social reality, and then collective action aimed at changing
individual and collective social realities are major thrusts of
social work practice that come from operationalization of empowerment, conscientization, and animation.

Whether social work is viewed as needing incorporation of a generalist, feminist, and social development-oriented practice in the form of a quiet radicalism, or of a loud radicalism possibly resulting in minor, moderate, or major reconstruction of social work, there are important implications for the profession, beginning with social work education. There is a need to assure that future students of the profession have more than a shallow mindhold on and commitment to the simultaneous dual focus and concern, the ultimate value and goal, the key generic concepts, and the principal mutually reinforcing practice approaches of social work that have been outlined. To achieve this, social work educators will need to deal with a problem that has grown more serious in the present neoconservative period, characterized by a moral ethic focused on individualism. Pearson put it this way: "Compared with the lavish care spent on helping students to develop casework and relationship skills, there is minimal effort to help them to relate to the complex personal, moral and political force-fields of social welfare."[52] To help rectify this situation, various spokespersons for the profession have recommended that schools of social work incorporate in their curricula, at minimum, a broader, richer, and better integrated knowledge of social theory, economic theory, and social policy; research concerned with both individual and institutional development; and organization, planning, and administration content organized with a systemic/structural focus.[53]

Conclusion

To sum up, social workers who lend their efforts almost exclusively to one side or the other of the equation of life, and engage in the social work so popular in many practice and academic settings today, are not offering what we consider an ultimate, distinctively professional social work contribution. The key to a reconstructed or reinvigorated practice lies with social workers who concertedly seek ways to link the subjective and objective dimensions of people's lives—both individual action and structural action—in a more comprehensive and creative combination than has ordinarily been the case up till now.

But there are powerful counterforces in the social structure,

in human personalities, and in the social work profession and
its educational programs as well, that make a more holistic
approach to the people-environment complex a vexing challenge. High moral purpose and visionary leadership in society
and in the profession are much in demand. The challenge before
social workers is to help not only others, but also themselves—
individually and corporately—to move to new levels of valuation of priorities, and then to new levels of thought and action.
This is anything but a simple process, for as Edgar Auerswald
has put it, many professionals would rather "fight than switch"
their present value orientation, cognitive style, and professional
way of life.[54] As Sperry has observed,

> In the majority of people most of the time immediate personal
> needs tend to dominate the value structure, and to suppress
> more transcendent values relating to the long-term good of
> . . . [hu]mankind as a whole. Only in the higher mental states
> that transcend immediate personal demands does one hope
> to find the kinds of value priorities needed today. . . .[55]

The answer to this challenge might be that more social
workers, and the profession as a whole, must begin to operate
from a recognition that the personal, political, psychological,
and structural aspects of life and, for that mater, of social work
practice are not so irredeemably incompatible and polarized as
our culture, language, practice settings, and educational institutions would have us believe. A reconstructed or reinvigorated
social work on the order proposed in this chapter, whether it be
quietly or loudly radical, is in essential accord with statements
about social work made by Halmos. He maintains that for social
workers ". . . a constant equibration between . . . [the "inner"
and "outer"] polarities is the sole response we can justify both
by logic and a humanistic moral philosophy."[56] And he has
added, "Only when the perspective is both personal and political can . . . [it] make a difference in the quality of life."

Notes

1. John Erlich, "The 'Turned On' Generation: New Anti-Establishment Action Roles," *Social Work* 16 (October 1971):22–27. Luis A.

Alfero, "Conscientization," in *New Themes in Social Work Education* (New York: International Association of Schools of Social Work, 1973), 72–81. Rosa P. Resnick, "Conscientization: an Indigenous Approach to International Social Work," *International Social Work* 19 (1976): 21–29. Marie R. Brun, "Animation and Social Work," in *New Themes in Social Work Education* (New York: International Association of Schools of Social Work, 1973), 60–71. Peninah A. Chilton et al., "Social Work Education: Radical Thought in Action," *Journal of Sociology and Social Welfare* 6 (1979):835–48; Ben Carniol, "Clash of Ideologies in Social Work Education," *Canadian Social Work Review '84* (Ottawa Ont.: Canadian Association of Schools of Social Work, 1984), 184–89. David Howe, *An Introduction to Social Work Theory* (Aldershot, Hauts, England: Wildwood House, 1987). David Wagner, "Radical Movements in the Social Services: A Theoretical Framework," *Social Service Review* 63 (1989):264–84.

2. Harold Throssell, ed., *Social Work: Radical Essays* (St. Lucia, Queensland, Australia: University of Queensland Press, 1975). Roy Bailey and Mike Brake, eds., *Radical Social Work* (New York: Pantheon Books, 1975). David G. Gil, *Beyond the Jungle: Essays on Human Possibilities, Social Alternatives and Radical Practice* (Boston: G. K. Hall, 1979). Jeffry Galper, ed., *Radical Social Work: Theory and Practice* (New York: MSS Modular Publications, 1980). Maurice Moreau and Lynne Leonard, *Empowerment Through a Structural Approach to Social Work* (Ottawa, Ont.: Carleton University School of Social Work, May 1989).

3. Michael Frumkin and Gerald O'Connor, "Where Has the Profession Gone? Where Is It Going?" *Urban and Social Change Review* 18 (Winter 1985):13–18.

4. See James E. Carigen, "The Case for Activism in Social Work" in *The Social Welfare Forum, 1972* (New York: Columbia University Press, 1972), 153–61. The quotation appears on p. 154. As he put it, "Too often, agency boundaries or some special person to be influenced—a supervisor, teacher, a colleague . . .—become the reasons for . . . [practitioners] limiting involvement to the more familiar and comfortable levels of direct treatment or crisis intervention. Often the client's need gets lost in this goal displacement process."

5. See Harold Throssell, "Social Work Overview" in *Social Work: Radical Essays* (St. Lucia, Queensland, Australia: University of Queensland Press, 1975), 3–25. The quotation appears on pp. 14–15. Exceptions to an undue practitioner concentration solely on the individual, of course, do arise. Rein has stated, "Not all social workers are prisoners of the collective status quo when they work with individuals. Many overtly and covertly resist these pressures. Resistance . . .

can . . . take several forms . . . [as] social workers try to activate those values that they accept as morally right and society accepts but fails to act on." See Rein, Martin, "Social Work in Search of a Radical Profession," *Social Work* 15 (April 1970):13–28. The quotation appears on pp. 21–22.

6. Noel Timms, *Social Work Values: An Enquiry* (London: Routledge & Kegan Paul, 1983), 91.

7. Frederic G. Reamer and Marcia Abramson, *The Teaching of Social Work Ethics* (Hastings-on-Hudson, N.Y.: The Hastings Center, 1982), viii.

8. Eduard C. Lindeman, "Science and Philosophy: Sources of Humanitarian Faith," in *Social Work as Human Relations* (New York: Columbia University Press, 1949), 220.

9. Howard Goldstein, "The Neglected Moral Link in Social Work Practice," *Social Work* 32 (May–June 1987):181–86. Max Siporin, "Deviance, Morality and Social Work Therapy," *Social Thought* 11 (1985) 4:11–24. Chris Clark, with Stewart Asquith, *Social Work and Social Philosophy: A Guide for Practice* (London: Routledge & Kegan Paul, 1985).

10. Howard Jones, *Towards a New Social Work* (London: Routledge & Kegan Paul, 1975), 65.

11. Geoffrey Pearson, "Making Social Workers: Bad Promises and Good Omens," in Roy Bailey and Mike Brake, eds., *Radical Social Work* (London: Edward Arnold, 1975), 15.

12. Robert S. Downie and Elizabeth Telfer, *Caring and Curing* (London: Methuen, 1980), 8.

13. John J. Hughes, "Toward a Moral Philosophy for Social Work," *Social Thought* 10 (1984) 15.

14. Siporin, "Deviance, Morality."

15. Harold Lewis, "Morality and the Politics of Practice," *Social Casework* 53 (1972):414.

16. Siporin, "Deviance, Morality;" idem, "Moral Philosophy in Social Work Today," *Social Service Review* 56 (1982):516–37.

17. Arthur J. Katz, "Directions for Social Work Practice: The Changing Contexts" in Kay Dea, ed., *Perspectives for the Future: Social Work Practice in the 80s* (Washington, DC: NASW, 1980), 53.

18. Siporin, "Ecological Systems Theory in Social Work," *Journal of Sociology and Social Welfare* 7 (1980):520–21.

19. Leslie Leighninger, "The Generalist-Specialist Debate in Social Work," *Social Service Review* 54 (1980):2.

20. Katherine A. Kendall, "No Quiet Place," *Reflections on Social Work Education, 1950–1978* (New York: International Association of Schools of Social Work, 1978), 108.

21. Muriel Pumphrey, "Transmitting Values and Ethics Through Social Work Practice," *Social Work* 6 (July 1961):75.

22. William E. Gordon, "A Critique of the Working Definition," *Social Work* 7 (October 1962):9.

23. William E. Gordon, "Unleashing the Social Work Potential." Paper presented at the St. Louis NASW Chapter meeting, 13 March 1963:2.

24. William E. Gordon, "The Fundamentals of Science in Social Work Education." Paper prepared for the Research Faculty Day Conference, Fourteenth Annual Program Meeting, Council on Social Work Education, New York, 28 January 1966:9–10.

25. William E. Gordon, "Fragmentation and Synthesis in Social Work Today," in Sue W. Spencer, ed., *Social Work: Promise and Pressures* (Nashville: The University of Tennessee School of Social Work, 1968), 8. Quoted Joseph Anderson, *Foundations of Social Work Practice* (New York: Springer Publishing Co., 1988), 8.

26. Anderson, *Foundations,* 8.

27. Daniel S. Sanders, Oscar Kurren, and Joel Fischer, eds., "Introduction," *Fundamentals of Social Work Practice* (Belmont, Calif.: Wadsworth Publishing Co., 1982), 1–14. Bradford Sheafor and Pam Landon, "Generalist Perspective," *Encyclopedia of Social Work,* vol. 1 (Silver Spring, Md., NASW, 1987), 660–69.

28. Karen S. Teigiser, "Evaluation of Education for Generalist Practice," *Journal of Education for Social Work* 19 (Winter, 1983):80.

29. Howard Goldstein, "Generalist Social Work Practice," in Neil Gilbert and Harry Specht, eds., *Handbook of the Social Services* (Englewood Cliffs, N.J.: Prentice-Hall, 1981), 433.

30. Nan Van Den Bergh and Lynn B. Cooper, "Introduction," in *Feminist Visions for Social Work* (Silver Spring, Md.: NASW, 1986), 1–28.

31. Carolyn Morell, "Cause *Is* Function: Toward a Feminist Model of Integration of Social Work," *Social Service Review* 61 (1987):147, 148.

32. Frank Paiva, "A Conception of Social Development," *Social Service Review* 51 (1977):327–36.

33. Irving Spergel, "The Role of the Social Developer" in Daniel S. Sanders, ed., *The Developmental Perspective in Social Work* (Manoa, University of Hawaii School of Social Work, 1982), 14.

34. John F. Jones, "Can We Teach Social Development in a Social Work Curriculum?" *International Social Work* 24 (1981):29–31.

35. Daniel S. Sanders, "People and Social Development Issues in the Pacific: A Challenge to the Social Work Profession," *International Social Work* 28 (1985):28.

36. Chauncey Alexander, "Professional Social Workers and Political Responsibility," in Maryann Mahaffey and John W. Hanks, eds., *Practical Politics: Social Work and Political Responsibility* (Silver Spring; Md.: NASW, 1982), 22.

37. Ibid, 22.

38. Howard Goldstein, "Generalist" 29, 431–32.

39. Ibid, 432.

40. Harry Specht, "Social Work and the Popular Psychotherapies," *Social Service Review* 64 (1990):345–57.

41. Edward E. Schwartz, "Social Work and Individualism: A Comparative Review," *Social Work* 34 (March, 1989):170.

42. Ibid.

43. Frederic G. Reamer, "Social Work and the Public Good: Calling or Career?" chapter 2 of this book.

44. Ibid.

45. See Max Siporin, "Practice Theory and Vested Interests," *Social Service Review* 52 (1978):418–36.

46. David Webb, "Themes and Continuities in Radical and Traditional Social Work," *British Journal of Social Work* 11 (1981):143–58.

47. Ibid., 150.

48. Leonard Schneiderman, "Social Welfare, Social Functioning, and Social Work: An Effort at Integration" in Robert W. Klenk and Robert Ryan, eds., *The Practice of Social Work*, 2nd ed. (Belmont, Calif.: Wadsworth Publishing Co., 1974), 366–67.

49. Michael Reisch, Stanley Wenocur, and Wendy Sherman, "Empowerment, Conscientization and Animation as Core Social Work Skills," *Social Development Issues* 5 (Summer/Fall 1981):108.

50. Ibid., 108.

51. Ibid., 109.

52. Pearson, "Making Social Workers" (note 11), 38.

53. Demetrius S. Iatridis, "New Social Deficit: Neoconservatism's Policy of Social Underdevelopment," *Social Work* 33 (January 1988): 11–15. Irving Spergel, "The Role of the Social Developer," 12–30. Gary A. Lloyd, "Social Development as a Political Philosophy: Implications for Curriculum Development in Social Work Education," in Sanders, *The Developmental Perspective*, 43–50.

54. Edgar Auerswald, "Interdisciplinary versus Ecological Approach," *Family Process*, 7 (September 1968): 202–25.

55. Roger Sperry, *Science and Moral Priority* (New York: Columbia University Press, 1983), 125.

56. Paul Halmos, *The Personal and the Political: Social Work and Political Action* (London: Hutchinson & Co., 1978), 19.

CHAPTER SEVEN

Competing Moral Values and Use of Social Work Authority with Involuntary Clients

Elizabeth D. Hutchinson

A homeless alcoholic is refusing shelter on a January evening when the temperature is in the subzero range. Should her social worker support a city ordinance that would require the sheltering of all homeless persons when the temperatures fall to a certain level? The intake worker at the local CPS agency has some suspicion that the caller who just filed a report of child neglect made the call out of spite. Should the worker make an investigative visit to the reported home? The social worker in a community-based corrections program has reason to believe a client with two previous "dirty" urine screenings is currently consuming illicit substances. Should the worker order another urinalysis, knowing that a third "dirty" screening is likely to send the client to prison? A disheveled, obviously hallucinating middle-aged man is brought to the hospital emergency room by the police because he has, in his rambling monologue, mentioned that God is directing him to kill some people. Should the emergency room social worker encourage involuntary commitment? An 85-year-old woman is lying on the floor with an apparent fractured hip when the home care social worker arrives, but she pleads with the worker not to call an ambulance because she hates hospitals and wants to die at home. Should the social worker call the ambulance anyway?

Social work, like other professions, must wrestle with its moral mission, and this book represents the ongoing effort of social work scholars to elucidate the moral philosophy of the profession. It is important to dissect the moral base of social work, but it is equally important to keep in mind that while you read this book, social workers are struggling with moral dilemmas like the ones described above. Probably no dilemmas present a greater challenge to social workers than decisions involving the use of social work authority with involuntary clients.[1]

> The particular ethical questions which concern social work reflect the special status of the profession as one whose practitioners are vested with various degrees of authority to intervene in the lives of individuals. . . . Several important questions derive from the "problem of authority." Under what circumstances are social workers obligated to intervene in the lives of others? What limits should we place on our interventions?[2]

Use of authority with involuntary clients poses such taxing problems for social workers because it involves competition among three values highly treasured by our profession—values of individual liberty, duty to aid vulnerable persons, and protection of the common good (public welfare). Each of these values will be described separately, followed by discussion of the disquieting dualisms among them. First, however, the rationale for the choice of competing moral values as an organizing framework for discussion of social work authority and involuntary clients is introduced.

Any analysis of the social structure of the United States emphasizes the plurality of our culture and the value multiplicity that flows from such plurality. The social welfare system is not isolated from this value multiplicity but, instead, reflects the value conflicts which exist in the culture. Tropman reminds us that the social welfare system is not built on a "neat, tidy, and unambiguous" value base.[3] On the contrary, social welfare programs approach their beneficiaries in several contradictory ways at the same time, because the value system contains support for different approaches. Tropman suggests, however, that there is a pattern of value conflicts in the culture which is reflected in the social welfare system. This pattern is dualism, or "conflict between two, opposed sets of values, with stress on one leading to a crisis in the other."[4] According to Tropman, almost any value in our culture can be opposed by another strongly held value. We tend to resolve these conflicts by developing a hierarchy of values, or by choosing which value will be designated *primus inter pares,* or first among equals.

Rappaport develops a similar concept using different language. He proposes that community life is by nature paradoxical and that antinomy, or contradiction between two equally binding or compelling laws, is the rule rather than the exception. In his view, we tend to resolve these pulls of opposite principles by emphasizing one to the relative exclusion of the other, often to become so unbalanced as to be forced to correct to the side of the opposite principle over time.[5]

Other social scientists have discussed this concept of competing values from a dialectical perspective. They see the development of the individual, as well as the development of the social world, as occurring through a process of synthesizing the push and pull of opposing forces. They, like Tropman and Rappaport, encourage us to see social problems as dialectical phenomena and, therefore, to recognize that our solutions will also involve a policy of paradox.[6]

Leiby proposes that social welfare programs in the United States have rested on three "general grounds": the legal doctrine of individual rights, the religious doctrine of charity, and the constitutional doctrine of police power. By police power, Leiby means the power of the state to protect the "health, safety, and morals of the community."[7] These "general grounds" of social welfare programs correspond to the competing moral values presented in this chapter as inherent in the use of social work authority with involuntary clients: Individual liberty, duty to aid vulnerable persons, and protection of the common good. The angst of delivering involuntary services springs, in the main, from two dualisms in these competing values: The dualism of individual liberty versus duty to aid vulnerable persons, and the dualism of individual liberty versus protection of the common good.

Individual Liberty

Personal autonomy is a core value in American law.[8] But autonomy, or individual liberty, is not simply a legal tenet; it is a deeply cherished value in the moral philosophy of Western societies. As McDermott suggests, ". . . the individual's right to make his own decisions and choices in matters affecting him, has long been regarded as one of the cornerstones of the moral framework to which democratic western societies are committed. . . ."[9] It would appear that individual liberty is considered, in Western cultures, to be not just *a* great moral value, but perhaps *the greatest* moral value. Hart suggests that there is one natural right, and that is the "equal right of all men to be free."[10]

Individual liberty is not a tidy moral concept. The tradition in moral philosophy is to conceptualize two forms of liberty—negative liberty and positive liberty. Negative liberty, simply stated, is the freedom not to be interfered with. Positive liberty refers not to this freedom from constraint, but to the active exercise of control over one's life.[11] Negative liberty is embedded in the American legal system and is the essence of the libertarian view. Positive liberty is synonymous with self-determination, meaning the effective determination of the course of one's life.

In a classic address entitled "Two Concepts of Liberty," Berlin proposes that although both types of liberty are to be valued, negative liberty is a higher moral ideal than positive liberty. Negative and positive liberty can, and often do, clash, Berlin suggests, but negative liberty is "fundamental" and the greatest harm to moral ideals occurs when negative liberty is violated.[12]

The ambiguities in moral philosophy about the conceptualization of individual liberty are reflected in the social work literature on self-determination. Is self-determination, a cherished social work value, to be understood as freedom from constraint, as the ability to self-direct one's life, or as some combination of these ideas? All three views have been presented in the social work literature.

Self-determination as negative liberty has been staunchly defended by McDermott, who recommends that

> the main function of the principle of client self-determination
> is to provide a moral restraint upon social workers in the
> pursuit of their professional aims; a moral restraint springing
> from the client's right to go his own way not because it is

constructive, good, or socially acceptable, but simply because it is his own.[13]

McDermott suggests that the concept of self-determination suffers under a steady attack by social workers who would like to define it as positive liberty. Some social workers submit, however, that a strict adherence to this negative liberty is inconsistent with the mission of social work to be instrumental in bringing about change in the interpersonal world.[14] These scholars, while not totally denying the value of freedom from constraint, have emphasized that a major function of social work is to stimulate clients' capacities for positive and constructive decision making—in order that they may be free in the positive sense to exercise control over their own lives. Some authors emphasize that constructive decision making includes responsible actions toward other persons.

Several social work scholars who have attempted to resolve the authority problem in relation to involuntary service provision have synthesized the negative and positive notions of liberty to define self-determination. Yelaja suggests that freedom has three components—the absence of external constraints, the ability and means to direct one's activities, and the power of conscious choice between significant, known alternatives.[15] Loewenberg and Dolgoff also propose that the client freedom which social workers speak of protecting is something more than the negative requirement not to interfere. According to these authors, freedom should be understood by social workers to include *all* of the following conditions: An environment that provides a set of options, lack of coercion from any source to choose an option, knowledge on the part of the client of all available options, accurate information on the costs of each option, capacity and/or initiative to make a choice, and realistic opportunity to act on the basis of the choice.[16]

Attempts to synthesize negative and positive concepts of freedom must contend, however, with the possibility that on occasion, negative and positive liberty may clash irreconcilably. The situations presented in the introduction to this chapter, of the homeless alcoholic, the hallucinating man, and the elderly woman with a fractured hip, are examples of such collisions of values. The dualism of individual liberty versus duty to aid vulnerable persons turns on the clash between negative and positive liberty. That dualism will be discussed later, but now it is time to discuss duty to aid as a value.

Duty to Aid Vulnerable Persons

Leiby reminds us that the initial rationale for social welfare programs was not related to individual liberty. It came instead from a religious emphasis on personal and social responsibility.[17] Salvation was ensured by the giving of alms.[18] Gradually, Western cultures moved from thinking in terms of individual acts of charity to expectations, albeit not uniformly held, that the state had a duty to aid and protect those in need.[19] Reamer recalls for us that the mission of social work was historically, and continues to be, based on the assumption that members of a society have an obligation to help those in need. Social workers, as a group, have also traditionally proposed that such caregiving could not practically be left to individuals or even voluntary associations, but that the state has a duty to assume a large share of the responsibility for overseeing the aid to persons in need. The social worker then becomes the expression of society's concern for the well-being of its sick, dependent, deprived, or deviant members.

For the first six and one-half decades of the twentieth century in the United States, duty to aid was translated into a model of the state as the caring parent.[20] This model, *parens patriae*, assumes that the state, like parents, acts benevolently or paternalistically in the best interests of the recipients of aid—those persons who cannot help themselves or cannot avoid harming themselves.[21]

For the last two decades, however, the notion of doing good has been under attack, and serious questions have been raised about the costs to negative liberty of our efforts to aid vulnerable persons. Rothman has suggested that "some paradox in our nature leads us, once we have made our fellow men the objects of our enlightened interest, to go on to make them the objects of our pity, then of our wisdom, ultimately of our coercion."[22] Many social workers have been stunned by the harsh reminder from the libertarians that duty to aid must always be acted on in the context of the dualism of individual liberty versus duty to aid. We will discuss protection of the common good before turning to that dualism.

Protection of the Common Good (Public Welfare)

Cultural anthropologists and the structural-functional sociologists emphasize that all societies must regulate the patterns of member behavior to ensure the minimal coordination required for survival of the social system.[23] They also suggest that as societies become more complex, they rely less on informal regulation to maintain order and must develop institutions to mediate the conflicting goals and competing demands for scarce resources.[24] Although social workers tend to be uncomfortable with the fact, societal sanction of the social work profession, and of social welfare programs, rests heavily on the understanding that social work is one of society's tools for securing conformity and controlling deviant individuals and groups.[25] Popple's discussion in chapter 8 reminds us of the conservative nature of the social function of social work.

Social workers who are comfortable with the value of protecting the public good would remind us, however, that professions like social work are essential to protect the social order—and that social order is the basis for each individual's freedom.[26] They would stress, as Gaylin has so articulately suggested, that "we do not choose to live in social relations; we are obliged to. It is this obligation to live in groups that renders the destruction of social living so dangerous, and makes neglect of the problems of public safety by the social and behavioral scientists so distressing."[27]

Social workers who are suspicious of the role of social work in protecting the common good ask the basic question: How can you talk about a "common" good in such a pluralistic world? Ultimately, will you not really be protecting the status quo and its hierarchy of wealth, prestige, and influence? Leonard has suggested that, in reality, social workers attempt to modify client behavior in the direction of middle-class values, practicing social control through social casework.[28] From this perspective social workers would stress the dualism between individual liberty and protection of the common good.

126

Individual Liberty versus Duty to Aid

Julian Rappaport has suggested that ". . . the paradoxical issue that demands our attention in the foreseeable future is a conflict between 'rights' and 'needs' models for viewing people in trouble."[29] This dualism of individual liberty versus duty to aid has certainly been the focus of much discussion during the last two decades. Several policy analysts have suggested that prior to the rights movements of the 1960s, the *parens patriae* doctrine of paternalistic state intervention was the compelling doctrine of the social welfare system, and little concern was expressed for controlling the power of the state to intervene.[30] Beginning in the late 1960s, however, a new generation of reformers, composed largely of lawyers and of members of dependent groups, began to draw attention to the conflict between rights and needs. They even began to challenge the political ideal of the state as caring parent. Rothman captured the spirit of the thrust of the rights movement when he commented,

> The commitment to paternalistic state intervention in the name of equality is giving way to a commitment to restrict intervention in the name of liberty. If our predecessors were determined to test the maximum limits for the exercise of the state power in order to correct imbalances, we are about to test the minimum limits for the exercise of state power in order to enhance autonomy.[31]

This dualism is currently manifested in a debate between a *parens patriae* orientation, sometimes associated with clinicians, and the civil libertarian orientation.

Those who present the *parens patriae* orientation emphasize that there will always be classes of persons—children, the physically and mentally infirm, persons temporarily incapacitated by substance abuse, etc.—who are not able to care for themselves or to avoid harming either themselves or others. These persons, it is argued, may not be able to ask for help, but may be relieved to have it mandated. This argument has been advanced particularly in regard to abusive parents, troubled adolescents, and offender clients.[32] It is also argued that although some involuntary clients resist assistance, their positive liberty may be enhanced by having assistance coerced. This has been the rationale for professionals who support involuntary commitment of psychiatric patients, coerced medication for psychiatric patients, and involuntary sheltering of homeless persons.[33] Rachlin summarizes this position well when speaking of involuntary commitment of psychiatric patients: ". . . I contend that the liberty to be psychotic is not freedom, and may represent the most restrictive alternative of all."[34] He would suggest that if the hallucinating man brought to the emergency room, in the example at the beginning of this chapter, is not hospitalized and does, indeed, proceed to kill someone, not only will he have harmed others, he will in fact have foreclosed on his own future freedom from interference. Professionals who support *parens patriae* as a moral doctrine suggest that the rationale for forced intervention rests on the belief that the outcome of client well-being is a higher value than client autonomy. This is a utilitarian rather than a deontological moral theory.

Civil libertarians, on the other hand, insist that the social welfare system that developed out of the Progressive fervor for intervention paid too much attention to "needs" and far too little attention to "rights."[35] They point to excesses and abuses that occurred in the name of intervention. Often-cited examples are midnight raids by caseworkers on the homes of mothers receiving aid to dependent children, excessive use of civil commitment, coerced medication for psychiatric patients,[36] and complete discretionary power of nursing homes over aged persons. The civil libertarians are concerned not only with the protection of individual liberty, but also with assuring that, when liberty must be abridged, due process is followed. Glasser suggests that "we must begin, at least legally, to mistrust service professionals as well as depend on them, much as we do the police."[37] In this view, the adversary system, with its procedural rights, helps to even the odds for vulnerable persons.

Professionals and administrators have criticized civil libertarian lawyers for elevating individual autonomy to such a level that both clients' need for treatment and society's need for protection are jeopardized.[38] Civil libertarians, on the other hand, have complained that professionals resist any attempts to limit their discretion, even though unlimited discretion by professionals can come only at the expense of their clients' rights.[38] Some civil libertarians have also suggested that coercive interventions might be more justifiable if professionals could ensure that no harm would be caused by these interventions. They argue that given the unconvincing track record of social service and mental health professionals, autonomy becomes even more important.[40]

Scholars who discuss this dilemma from the perspective of competing values recognize that the rights movement was necessary to remind us of the dualism of individual liberty and duty to aid—that we had developed a naive faith that benevolence can do no harm and some correction was necessary. Now it appears that we have corrected too far to the "rights" side of the duality, and that we are currently at risk of sacrificing services to the point that we can protect neither "rights" nor "needs." Our current challenge is to use both voices to forge a social policy that is decent and caring without being unnecessarily coercive.

Some social work scholars have relied on the moral philosopher Alan Gewirth to develop guidelines for decision making involving the dualism of individual liberty and duty to aid.[41] Gewirth sought a supreme moral principle to resolve competing moral values. This search led him to the Principle of Generic Consistency: "Act in accord with the generic rights of your recipients as well as of yourself."[42] Gewirth identifies two generic rights—voluntariness and well-being. These two generic rights correspond to the "rights" and "needs" views of social welfare policy discussed above. According to Gewirth, all persons have a moral imperative to act in such a way as to protect their own freedom and well-being, as well as the freedom and well-being of other persons. It does not escape Gewirth's attention, however, that this principle does not resolve moral dilemmas between individual liberty and duty to aid. A second principle is developed to assist with these dilemmas, the Principle of Proportionality: "The degree to which different groups approach having the generic features and abilities of action determines the degree to which they have or approach having the generic rights."[43] As an example of this principle, Gewirth suggests that mentally deficient persons do not have *to the same degree* the right to freedom that other adults have, because they lack the "basic goods" to exercise control over their behavior.

Gewirth raises the question of degree, the stickiest question for providers of services to involuntary clients. Most social service professionals are comfortable with the notion that they must provide aid in accord with the right to well-being, but the hard questions are, at what point of well-being do you provide aid, and how do you best intervene in accordance with the right to freedom? Where does the authority of the professional leave off and the rights of the client take over? In the early days of the rights movement dangerousness was the criterion used by the legal system to warrant coercive intervention.[44] As it became evident that we had insufficient knowledge to predict dangerousness, civil libertarians seized on the idea that "recent acts" were the best criteria to predict present and future dangerousness.

Recently, however, it seems that even many rights activists have become concerned about the possibility that the libertarian view can be used to promote neglect—which constitutes cruelty to dependent persons. After thoughtful consideration of the competing values of individual liberty and duty to aid, Marcus concludes, that ". . . we can degrade people by caring for them; and we can degrade them by not caring for them, and in matters such as these there are neither simple answers nor simple solutions."[45] Although the answers are not simple, we can develop social work practice principles that respect the complexity of the competing values.

Individual Liberty versus Protection of the Common Good

The United States Constitution and its amendments were drafted out of a deep-seated fear of the "Totalitarian Menace."[46] Tropman suggests that this distrust of centralized external control of individual liberty may be a primary reason that the United States was slow to develop a national program of social welfare. He notes, however, that Americans are unique in valuing both freedom and control, commenting that "the American character faces constant conflict between permission and control."[47] Paradoxically, it is our love of liberty that makes us recognize that liberties can be exercised only when a system of social control "limits, protects, and enhances the boundaries of individual freedom."[48]

Given the culture's ambivalence about the values of individual freedom and social control for the protection of the common good, it is small wonder that social workers often feel severe role strain in regard to these values. Social work is unique among professions for its stated commitment to represent both the individual and the social welfare in each intervention. Some have called this a dual focus; others have emphasized the inseparability of humans from their environments and have suggested that our central purpose is to "effect the best possible adaptation among individuals, groups, and their environments."[49] The legal profession also aims to resolve conflicts that arise when individual interests clash, but attorneys operate in an adversarial system which requires that they represent only one interest at a time. Social workers have traditionally taken a mediation stance as opposed to an adversarial stance.

Cumming has suggested that "... to be at once on the client's side and on the side of society can involve intolerable role strain."[50] On many occasions, individual welfare and the interests of the community may appear to conflict. For example, the chronic psychiatric patient may prefer treatment "in the community," but several neighborhoods have rejected community residences. It is exactly such situations, however, that require professionals who can tolerate the ambiguities of the dualism of individual liberty and protection of the common good. A social worker's responsibility is to "heal broken social relationships"[51] and that cannot be accomplished, in many instances, if the social worker identifies too closely either with the client against the rules and norms of the community, or with the formal authority of the community, especially if it is unjust.

Philosophers remind us that although societies cannot survive without institutionalized authority, such authority "... by its very nature, must have a built-in tendency to exclude the dynamic and thrusting innovator."[52] From this perspective, social systems grow and develop by tension between institutionalized authority and emergent authority. Social workers must be wary of becoming so aligned with institutionalized authority as to assist in the maintenance of an unjust or stagnant order.

Civil libertarians acknowledge that the welfare of society must sometimes take precedence over the rights of a particular individual, but they argue that the decision must be a legal one, with full attention to due process. Such decisions, they insist, should not be left in the hands of social service and mental health professionals.[53] The civil libertarian stance over the past two decades, despite many problems in implementation, is that the only justification for coercive intervention is serious harm to others—the concept of dangerousness. As Rosenblatt suggests, civil libertarians hold tight to two principles that, when implemented, may protect individual liberty at the cost of public safety. The first of these principles is that it is preferable to find ten criminals innocent than to find one innocent person guilty. The second principle is that preventive detention of persons *suspected* of endangering public safety is a violation of their individual liberties.[54]

In recent years increasing numbers of social work scholars have complained that the libertarian view has inappropriately become the most cherished social work value.[55] These scholars elaborate on Bernstein's thesis that "it is a strange kind of ethic that elevates the desire of the client above those to whom he is socially related."[56] Some authors also emphasize that the common good should not be interpreted narrowly as public safety, but should include the morals of the community as represented in the original concept of police power.[57] In this view social workers must serve as a conscience, to assist the client to contemplate social obligations and duties as much as rights and entitlements.[58] Siporin insists that we need moral theory that understands persons as "interrelated human beings in real-life situations."[59] Both Falck and Siporin complain that the libertarian view rests on individualistic psychology; Siporin considers this a deficient perspective, while Falck considers it an inaccurate perspective. Concern over the growing supremacy of a libertarian view has led to preliminary attempts to reconstruct the moral base of social work on the collectivist rather than the liberalist doctrine.

Collectivism as an Organizing Principle for Social Work

Reamer reminds us in chapter 1 that the United States, like other Western cultures, adopted liberalism as political doctrine rather than choosing the rival doctrine of collectivism or socialism. In so doing we rejected the collaborative theories embedded in Christian socialism, Marxist socialism, and the Eastern religions. Keith Graham has argued for a greater recognition of collective entities[60] in moral philosophy, but Tropman suggests that "political or social theories that tend to . . . deemphasize the prominence of the individual have not been widely accepted in American society, though individualism has its critics, too."[61] Although several social work scholars have criticized social work's one-sided emphasis on individualism and autonomy, two recent attempts to revise the base of social work to a more collectivist vision are notable. One comes from feminist social workers and the other from Hans Falck's membership model.

Feminist social workers, drawing on work by feminist psychologists, have in recent years emphasized a need to focus on connectedness rather than estrangement. They propose that social work be built on a "feminine ethics of interdependence, relational commitment, and a morality that encompasses the realities of mutual compassion and care."[62] Gillian Dalley, a British feminist, takes this position a step further by tracing the principle of collectivism, historically and anthropologically, even in Western societies. She submits that our current emphasis on individualizing and privatizing social life and social welfare programs is a source of serious danger to dependent persons and their female caregivers. She proposes a reconceptualization that rests on the principle of collective responsibility for dependent persons. She contrasts this approach to our current reliance on principles of familism and possessive individualism.[63]

Falck, in the introduction to his membership perspective on social work, states explicitly that this perspective "rejects individualism and all of its concepts."[64] Falck does not reify the social world, either, and he is clear that he would not call his model collectivist. His model does rest, however, on the assumption of inseparability of the member from the group, an assumption that characterizes a variety of collectivist or socialist doctrines. Falck redefines the purpose of social work practice as rendering professional aid in the management of membership.[65]

From the perspective of competing moral values, attempts to revise the moral base of social work toward a collectivist end were inevitable, given the exaggerated emphasis on individual liberty that developed out of the rights movement. As Tropman suggests, however, these revisions will swim upstream in a society that, while holding multiple conflicting values, has a strong tradition of placing individual liberty first in the hierarchy of values.

Falck must contend with the same criticism leveled against Marxist socialism: He appears to assume a social order based primarily on integration, consensus, and solidarity. Those who want to practice social work from a more radical paradigm emphasize structural conflict, patterns of domination, and oppression—and suggest that we cannot dispense with the notion of individual rights as long as the world in which we live is driven by egoistic motives. Such concerns are answerable within the membership perspective, but need to be addressed more specifically. Falck states ". . . membership under conditions of social justice implies obligation."[66] Further development of the model should address the question, what does membership imply under conditions of social injustice? That question troubles many social workers, particularly those in coercive settings, as they decide when and how to use their authority with involuntary clients.

Conclusion

The issue is not whether to use social work authority to protect the well-being of individuals and their collectivities—but "when, how, to what degree, and with what safeguards to client, worker"[67] and community. Authority exists in every sphere of human life, but authority is not absolute; it must be justified by its prior achievements, its current ideals, and its postulates about the future.[68] Social work, like the nation state, must base its use of authority on a moral philosophy.

The moral base for use of social work authority with involuntary clients involves competing moral values. The central thesis of this chapter is that the need to make choices among highly treasured values is endemic to social life, and therefore to the professions which try to enhance that social life. It does us no good, indeed, it does great harm to deny the push and pull of opposing forces of rights, needs, public safety, and collective health. It is far better to face intellectually the complexity of the decisions to be made, and to recognize that most decisions violate some cherished value. We have seen the results of unbridled and often punitive emphasis on needs, followed by exaggerated emphasis on rights, and neither alternative is attractive. Nor is our problem solved by replacing an exaggerated individualist perspective with an exaggerated collectivist perspective. Both present the possibility for oppression. Social workers must manage the push and pull of connectedness and separateness inherent in social life.

Social work authority is safe only in the hands of professionals who can wrestle conscientiously with the ambiguities of social life. To assist in navigating these ambiguities, social work practitioners need guidelines for the use of social work authority with involuntary clients that recognize the complexity of the competing values at stake. The author has presented a working draft of such practice principles elsewhere,[69] but some of these principles deserve elaboration in light of the present discussion.

When balancing individual liberty and duty to aid, the social worker must assess, with maximum client input, the dimensions of freedom suggested by Lowenberg and Dolgoff: the existing options, the sources of coercion and constraints on decision making, the client's knowledge of existing options and their benefits and costs, the client's capacity and/or initiative to make a choice, and the opportunities for action.[70] The social worker should use authority, in its various forms, to influence the client to make the most informed choice possible. Coercive interventions to protect the client's well-being should occur only if clear evidence demonstrates that the client lacks either the cognitive or emotional resources to make rational, informed decisions. When coercive interventions are deemed necessary, the client should be advised of the competing values involved and the reasons for the decision to intervene against the client's wishes. This information should, of course, be offered at a level the client can understand, but should be offered even if it appears the client will not comprehend it.

When balancing the values of individual liberty and protection of the common good, the social worker should use authority to influence the client to recognize his or her social nature and social obligations. The social worker should also acknowledge with the client any sources of social injustice that render the client's membership in social groups problematic. The social worker should lend support to all professional efforts to alter unjust social structures. Coercive interventions for the purposes of protecting the common good should be utilized in only two types of situations: to fulfill a contract with the client or a contract with agency or state about which the client was fully informed, *or* if evidence demonstrates that the client represents a danger to another person.

Practice principles such as the ones outlined above will not turn complex social phenomena into simple ones, but they will assist social workers to tolerate the ambiguities of competing moral values when using social work authority with involuntary clients. Increased knowledge and skill will not eliminate the need to wrestle with the underlying competing moral values involved in providing involuntary services. Moral dilemmas in social work will always mirror the competing values of the political philosophy of the existing culture.

Notes

1. Elizabeth D. Hutchinson, "Use of Authority in Direct Social Work Practice with Mandated Clients," *Social Service Review* 61 (1987):581–98.

2. Frederic G. Reamer, *Ethical Dilemmas in Social Service* (New York: Columbia University Press, 1982), 42.

3. John E. Tropman, *American Values and Social Welfare: Cultural Contradictions in the Welfare State* (Englewood Cliffs, N.J.: Prentice-Hall, 1989), 20.

4. Ibid., 21.

5. Julian Rappaport, "In Praise of Paradox: A Social Policy of Empowerment Over Prevention," in Edward Seidman and Julian Rappaport, eds., *Redefining Social Problems* (New York: Plenum Press, 1986).

6. See, e.g., W. Graham Astley and Andrew H. Van de Ven, "Central Perspectives and Debates in Organization Theory," *Administrative Science Quarterly* 28 (1983):245–73. J. Kenneth Benson, "Organizations: A Dialectical View," *Administrative Science Quarterly* 22 (1977): 1–19. R. Edwards, "The Competing Values Approach as an Integrating Framework for the Management Curriculum," *Administration in Social Work* 11 (1987):1–13. Klaus F. Riegel, "Toward a Dialectical Theory of Development," *Human Development* 18 (1975):50–64. Andrew H. Van de Ven and W. Graham Astley, "Mapping the Field to Create a Dynamic Perspective on Organization Design and Behavior," in Andrew H. Van de Ven and William F. Joyce, eds., *Perspectives on Organizational Design and Behavior* (New York: John Wiley, 1981), 427–68.

7. James Leiby, "Moral Foundations of Social Welfare and Social Work: A Historical View," *Social Work* 30 (July/August, 1985):323.

8. John Petrila, "Mandated Services: Legal Issues," in Aaron Rosenblatt, ed., *For Their Own Good: Essays in Coercive Kindness* (Albany, N.Y.: Nelson A. Rockefeller Institute of Government, 1988).

9. F. E. McDermott, "Introduction," in F. E. McDermott, ed., *Self-Determination in Social Work* (Boston: Routledge & Kegan Paul, 1975), 2.

10. H.L.A. Hart, "Are There Any Natural Rights?" F.E. McDermott, ed., in *Self-Determination in Social Work* (Boston: Routledge & Kegan Paul), 192.

11. See, e.g., Isaiah Berlin, *Four Essays on Liberty* (New York: Oxford University Press, 1970). Leiby, "Moral Foundations." H. J. McCloskey, "A Critique of the Ideals of Liberty," *Mind* 74 (October 1965):483–508. Charles Taylor, "What's Wrong with Negative Liberty," in *The Idea of Freedom*, ed. Alan Ryan (New York: Oxford University Press, 1979).

12. Isaiah Berlin, "Two Concepts of Liberty," in *Four Essays on Liberty* 118–72.

13. F. E. McDermott, "Against the Persuasive Definition of Self-Determination," in McDermott, *Self-Determination* 136.

14. See, e.g., Felix P. Biestek, "Client Self-Determination," in McDermott, *Self-Determination*, 17–32. Saul Bernstein, "Self-Determination: King or Citizen in the Realm of Values?" *Social Work* 5 (January 1960):3–8. Peter R. Day, *Social Work and Social Control*

(New York: Tavistock Publications, 1981). Robert Foren and Royston Bailey, *Authority in Social Casework* (Oxford: Pergamon Press, 1968).

15. Shankar A. Yelaja, "Freedom and Authority," in Shankar A. Yelaja, ed., *Authority and Social Work: Concept and Use* (Toronto: University of Toronto Press, 1971), 37.

16. Frank Loewenberg and Ralph Dolgoff, *Ethical Decisions for Social Work Practice*, 2nd ed. (Itasca, Ill.: F.E. Peacock Publishers, 1985), 24.

17. Leiby, "Moral Foundations."

18. Carel B. Germain and Alex Gitterman, *The Life Model of Social Work Practice* (New York, Columbia University Press, 1980), 345.

19. Reamer, *Ethical Dilemmas*, 43.

20. See, e.g., Petrila, "Mandated Services." Rappaport, "In Praise." David Rothman, "Introduction," Willard Gaylin, Ira Glasser, Steven Marcus, and David Rothman, eds., *Doing Good: The Limits of Benevolence* (New York: Pantheon, 1981).

21. Petrila, "Mandated Services."

22. David Rothman, "The State as Parent: Social Policy in the Progressive Era," in Gaylin et al., *Doing Good*, 72.

23. See, e.g., Talcott Parson, "Evolutionary Universals in Society," *American Sociological Review* 2 (1964):339–57. Edith M. Tufts, "Psychological Authority: An Operational Definition for Social Work," in Yelaja, *Authority and Social Work*, 90–97.

24. Elaine Cumming, *System of Social Regulation* (New York: Atherton Press, 1968). Day, *Social Work and Social Control*. Emile Durkheim, *The Division of Labor in Society*, trans. George Simpson (New York: Macmillan, 1947), 24.

25. See, e.g., Richard Cloward and Frances Fox Piven, *Regulating the Poor* (New York: Pantheon, 1971). Irving Weisman and Jacob Chwast, "Control and Values in Social Work Treatment," in Yelaja, *Authority and Social Work*, 196–205. Colin Whittington, "Self-Determination Reexamined," in McDermott, *Self-Determination*, 81–92.

26. See, e.g., Day, *Social Work and Social Control*. Foren and Bailey, *Authority*. Max Siporin, "Moral Philosophy in Social Work Today," *Social Service Review* 56 (December 1982):516–38.

27. Willard Gaylin, "In the Beginning: Helpless and Dependent," in Gaylin, *Doing Good*, 34.

28. Peter Leonard, "Social Control, Class Values and Social Work Practice," *Social Work* [U.K.] 22 (October 1965):9–13.

29. Rappaport, "In Praise," 141.

30. See, e.g., Gaylin, *Doing Good*. Petrila, "Mandated Services."

Stephen Rachlin, "The Limits of *Parens Patriae*," in Rosenblatt, *For Their Own Good*, 1–14. Aaron Rosenblatt, "Involuntary Civil Commitment," in *For Their Own Good*, 163–205. Rothman, "The State."

31. Rothman, "The State," 73–74.

32. See, e.g., Chester I. Barnard, "The Theory of Authority," in Yelaja, *Authority*, 48–64. Bernstein, "Self-Determination." Judith E. Gourse and Martha W. Chescheir, "Authority Issues in Treating Resistant Clients," *Social Casework* 62 (1981), 67–73. Sally Palmer, "Authority: An Essential Part of Practice," *Social Work* 28 (March–April 1983), 120–25.

33. See, e.g., Rachlin, "The Limits." Rappaport, "In Praise." Rosenblatt, "Involuntary Civil Commitment."

34. Rachlin, "The Limits," 1.

35. See, e.g., Ira Glasser, "Prisoners of Benevolence: Power versus Liberty in the Welfare State," in Gaylin et al., *Doing Good*, 99–170. Petrila, "Mandated Services." Rothman, "The State," 35.

36. Kia J. Bentley, "The Right of Psychiatric Patients to Refuse Medication: Where Should Social Workers Stand?" Paper presented at the Annual Meeting of the National Association of Social Workers, San Francisco, 1990.

37. Glasser, "Prisoners," 127.

38. See, e.g., Rappaport, "In Praise." Rosenblatt, "Involuntary Civil Commitment."

39. Glasser, "Prisoners," 127.

40. Ibid.

41. Loewenberg and Dolgoff, *Ethical Decisions*. Reamer, *Ethical Dilemmas*.

42. Alan Gewirth, *Reason and Morality* (Chicago: University of Chicago Press, 1978), 135.

43. Ibid., 141.

44. Petrila, "Mandated Services."

45. Steven Marcus, "Their Brothers' Keepers: An Episode from English History," in Gaylin et al. *Doing Good*, 65–66.

46. Taylor, "What's Wrong," 179.

47. Tropman, *American Values*, 39.

48. Sidney Z. Moss, "Authority—An Enabling Factor in Casework with Neglectful Parents," *Child Welfare* (October 1963):385–91.

49. Carol Meyer, "Direct Practice in Social Work: Overview," in *Encyclopedia of Social Work*, 18th ed. (Silver Spring, Md., NASW, 1987), 409.

50. Cumming, *Systems of Social Regulation*, 409.

51. Elliot Studt, "An Outline for Study of Social Authority Factors in Casework," *Social Casework* 35 (1954), 236.

52. Stanley I. Benn, "Authority," in Paul Edwards, ed., *The Encyclopedia of Philosophy* (New York: Macmillan, 1967), 216.

53. Petrila, "Mandated Services."

54. Rosenblatt, "Involuntary Civil Commitment," 169.

55. Hans Falck, *Social Work: The Membership Perspective* (New York: Springer Publishing Co., 1988). Leiby, "Moral Foundations." Siporin, "Moral Philosophy."

56. Bernstein, "Self-Determination."

57. Leiby, "Moral Foundations."

58. See, e.g., Bernstein, "Self-Determination." Falck, *Social Work.* Siporin, "Moral Philosophy."

59. Siporin, "Moral Philosophy," 532.

60. Keith Graham, "Morality, Individuals, and Collectives," in J.D.G. Evans, ed., *Moral Philosophy and Contemporary Problems* (New York: Cambridge University Press), 1–18.

61. Tropman, *American Values,* 11.

62. Barbara G. Collins, "Defining Feminist Social Work," *Social Work* 31 (May–June 1986):216.

63. Gillian Dalley, *Ideologies of Caring: Rethinking Community and Collectivism* (London: Macmillan Education, 1988).

64. Falck, *Social Work,* xvii.

65. Ibid., 56.

66. Ibid, 192.

67. Edna Wasser, "Responsibility, Self-Determination, and Authority in Casework Protection of Older Persons," in Yelaja, *Authority,* 190.

68. James Iverach, "Authority," in James Hastings, ed., *Encyclopedia of Religion and Ethics* (New York: Charles Scribner's Sons, 1951), 249–54.

69. Hutchinson, "Use of Authority."

70. Loewenberg and Dolgoff, "Ethical Decisions."

CHAPTER EIGHT

Social Work: Social Function and Moral Purpose

Philip R. Popple

The lead paper in this volume discusses whether social work is, or should be, a calling or a career. This, along with most of the other papers here, is merely the most recent in a long line of papers addressing social work's dualistic nature. We have had references to this dualism as retail and wholesale, cause and function, social work and social welfare, service and movement, social and psychological, services and welfare, compassion and protection, among others. These dualisms have been given different names and subjected to a variety of treatments, but they all boil down to the same basic questions. These questions involve, on one side, whether social work should concentrate on social or on individual change and on the other, whether social workers should be objective professionals more or less dispassionately carrying out a technical social function or partisan, selfless crusaders for various social causes. Toren has referred to the profession's dualistic nature as "the dilemma of social work," and argues that the result has been that social work has developed as a profession with a dual focus, a situation which she views as dysfunctional.[1] Chambers has noted that "Between the 'movers and the shakers' on the one hand, and the 'seekers and sojourners' on the other, there has often been misunderstanding and bad blood."[2]

A Brief History of Social Work Dualisms

It seems as though each generation of social workers must, on its own, rediscover and wrestle with the issue of the dualistic nature of the profession. In 1905, before the term "social work" was even in common usage, the great caseworker Mary Richmond indicated her awareness of the duality of the profession and her acceptance of it as natural. She referred to the "retail" aspects of social work, direct services to individuals for the purpose of solving individual problems, and its "wholesale" aspects, large-scale reform movements to deal with problems shared by whole groups of people. She wrote, "The healthy and well-rounded reform movement usually begins in the retail method and returns to it again, forming in the two curves of its upward push and downward pull a complete circle." In 1923 she again recognized this duality, and its appropriateness and desirability, when she stated that she would probably spend the remainder of her career convincing people that "casework is not all there is to social work."[3]

Porter R. Lee gave what is perhaps the most famous and influential treatment of social work's dual nature in 1929, when he spoke of social work as "cause" and "function." Lee agreed with Richmond that the duality was natural and inevitable, and that the two aspects were complementary. He looked at the problem in an evolutionary fashion. Lee argued that a cause, once successful, naturally tended to "transfer its interest and its responsibility to an administrative unit" which justified its existence by the test of efficiency, not zeal; by its "demonstrated possibilities of achievement" rather than by the "faith and purpose of its adherents." The emphasis of the function was upon "organization, technique, standards, and efficiency." Fervor inspired the cause, and intelligence directed the function. Lee felt that once the cause was won, it had to be institutionalized as a function in order to make its gains permanent. This he saw as the primary aim of professional social work.[4]

In 1929 Lee was concerned with demonstrating how social work as a profession (a function) differed from concern and action in response to general social welfare problems (causes). In 1958 Burns turned the table, and expounded on the same subject from the perspective of the National Conference of Social Welfare. This group had changed its name from the National Conference of Social Work in 1956, and was attempting to establish itself as an interdisciplinary interest group rather than a professional organization. Burns observed that the tendency to restrict "social work" to denote a specific group of social welfare measures and a specific series of skilled services has been hastened by the development of a profession of social workers who, like all professionals, are inevitably interested in establishing their professional identity and sphere of competence and monopoly . . . The professional objective is, understandably, performance as an individual, at the highest levels of professional competence.

Burns agreed with Lee that "function" was the appropriate role of social work. She argued that a highly organized social work profession could not be effective in dealing with large social issues, saying, "In social welfare this emphasis on maximizing professional performance has had results little short of disastrous."[5]

In 1963 Schwartz wrote of service and movement, basically a restating and reaffirming Lee's cause and function argument. Schwartz argued that professions grow out of social movements, and that, "As this effort begins to achieve some success, and as the group and its cause begin to take on some stability and permanence within the social division of labor, the concerns of the profession undergo a gradual shift from the problems of social *advocacy* to those of social *effectiveness*."[6]

In the 1960s and 1970s, as society entered a liberal reform phase, the literature began to reflect a growing sentiment that perhaps the ideas of people like Lee, Burns, and Schwartz were wrong. Roy Lubove, a historian on the faculty of the University of Pittsburgh School of Social Work, argued that social workers should deemphasize their traditional service role and become hawks instead of doves. He advised social workers to "confront the hard questions of power and income redistribution." Frankel criticized social work for "tinkering with the broken products that are brought to the repair shop," without asking "why so many of these broken products have been brought in." Gilbert and Specht asserted that social work was an incomplete profession because it had developed a commitment to services, and not to welfare.[7]

Although the social change versus individual treatment question has been the most obvious and most discussed dualism in social work, there have occasionally been others of interest. One is Pumphrey's description of compassion and protection as dual motivations in social welfare. Pumphrey argued that all social welfare is driven by two more or less compatible motives. On the one side is the desire of people to make the lives of others better. "This aspect of philanthropy may be designated as *compassion*: the effort to alleviate present suffering, deprivation, or other undesirable conditions to which a segment of the population, but not the benefactor, is exposed." On the other side are programs designed for the benefit of their promoters and of the community at large. Pumphrey called this motivation *protection* and stated that, "It may result either from fear of change or from fear of what may happen if existing conditions are not changed." Pumphrey concludes by offering the hypothesis that social welfare institutions which have proven effective have been characterized by a balance between compassion and protection.[8]

The interesting question is why social work is continually discussing its own dualistic nature. An obvious answer, and the one most frequently given, is that social work by definition deals with person-in-situation, a dualistic phenomena. But there is more to it, and the answer has to do with social work's moral purposes. I suggest that the fundamental dualism in social work, the one from which all others are derived, has to do with a mismatch between the social function of social work as a profession within the social welfare institution and the individual motivations of the people who enter it. This mismatch was first implied in 1892 by Jane Addams, when she spoke of the subjective necessity for the social settlements.

Social Work's Objective and Subjective Necessity

In 1892 Jane Addams attended a summer school at Plymouth, Massachusetts, sponsored by the Ethical Culture Societies for the purpose of addressing the general theme of "Philanthropy and Social Progress." Addams's contribution to this event was a paper titled "The Subjective Necessity for Social Settlements." An unstated assumption in Addams's paper is that there was an objective necessity for the settlements, one that generally formed the rationale for their existence. This objective necessity was based on the familiar litany of late-nine-teenth-century urban problems—immigration, Americaniza-tion, industrial accidents, sanitation, poverty, communicable diseases, child labor, and so on. These were problems which needed to be managed in order for society to survive. Settle-ments contributed to this management, hence their objective necessity. The actual subject of the paper, however, derived mainly from Addams's own experience, described the need of her generation of young people, particularly young women, to do something meaningful with their lives. She summarized this "subjective necessity" as a combination of three trends: "first, the desire to interpret democracy in social terms; secondly, the impulse beating at the very source of our lives, urging us to aid in the race progress; and, thirdly, the Christian movement toward humanitarianism."[9] Lasch has observed that the settle-ments provided people like Addams and her colleague Ellen Gates Starr with ". . . a secular outlet . . . for energies essentially religious. It is commonplace to say that progressivism repre-sented another outcropping of the old New England moralism. Such observations are quite misleading, however, unless cou-pled with the observation that the old moralism now existed in a theological void."[10] For Addams, then, the subjective neces-sity of the settlements was their moral purpose.

Addams was writing in 1892. Does her essay have any relevance for the 1990s? I think it does. Modern social work has an objective and a subjective necessity, just as in Addams's day. The objective necessity has something to do with the social function of social work as a profession. The subjective necessity involves the motivations, based on values, of the individuals who enter the profession.

The Objective Necessity—The Nature of Professions and the Social Function of Social Work

I have argued elsewhere that social work has been poorly served by the sociology of the professions.[11] Sociologists, and the social workers who read them, have paid far too much attention to people like Flexner and Greenwood who basically attempted to describe what traits differentiated professions from lesser careers in our society.[12] The far more interesting and useful, though largely ignored, work of Max Weber dealt with the *function* of professions in modern society rather than with what professions look like. In the work of Weber we find an explanation of the objective necessity for professions in general.[13] His work can be extended to explain the function of the social work profession in particular.

Weber was interested in the differences between modern and premodern societies. He observed that one major difference was modern society's pursuit of rationality, and this constituted the focus of his work. Weber regarded three structures as personifications of rationality—the market, bureaucracy, and professionalism. The conditions that lead to a rational choice between bureaucratic and professional organization of work relate to the nature of the task to be performed. Complex work can be undertaken by either bureaucratic or professional organizations. When work is routine and can be standardized and controlled by external supervision, bureaucratic organization is the most rational form. For complex, non-routine decision making which requires control mechanisms internal to the worker, professionalism is regarded as the most rational manner of organization.[14]

Jamous and Peloille have proposed an interesting definition, based on Weber's work, of the function of professions. They say that although any productive activity implies a measure of indetermination, professions are "occupations . . . whose indetermination/technicality ratio, intrinsic to the systems of production, is generally high." Whereas technicality represents "means that can be mastered and communicated in the form of rules," indetermination covers "means that escape rules and, at a given historical moment, are attributed to the virtualities of the producers."[15] In other words, bureaucratization is the most efficient form of work organization if the tasks to be performed can be standardized. As soon as the work performed becomes too complex for routinization in the form of rules, it is necessary to substitute for external control a form of control internalized by the workers. At this point jobs become professions, because it is only through professional education, socialization, codes of ethics, etc., that internal control mechanisms can be developed.

Thus, professions emerge because they perform a necessary function (i.e., an objective necessity) for a society which prizes rationality. If social work is a profession, and there is every reason to argue that it is, what is its function? A useful attempt to answer this question was presented by Atherton in a 1969 article, and elaborated upon by Cowger and Atherton in 1974.[16] Atherton conceptualizes social work's social function as the control of dependency in society. He defines dependency as "a state of being in which one is not able to carry on with the business of living in his culture by use of his own resources, skills, abilities, and knowledge. The dependent person, then, is one who needs resources that enable him to perform legitimate social roles that he is not now performing satisfactorily either in his own judgment or in the judgment of society."[17] In preindustrial society, dependency was not a great problem because it was handled by the family, church, and community. As societies developed and industrialized, these institutions began to break down, and dependency became a serious problem. Atherton argues that "when the industrial society recognized dependency as a threatening state of affairs, it evolved a social mechanism—a technology or profession—to deal with it."[18] In other words, during the late nineteenth century a problem emerged that threatened Western society: dependency. The handling of dependency is too complex and non-routine to be dealt with bureaucratically, so the management of it was defined as "professional." The profession which emerged to fulfill this objective necessity is, of course, social work.

Thus, the objective necessity for social work is society's need to manage dependency. Cowger and Atherton observe with some dismay that social workers see something vaguely sinister in the notion of social control. This is an accurate observation. However, Cowger and Atherton argue that this discomfort reflects a basic misunderstanding of the real purposes of social control. I argue that social workers understand social control perfectly well, they just don't like it. Just as settlement workers in Addams's day entered the work from a subjective necessity different from the objective necessity, today's social workers choose their careers from motivations which are often at odds with the profession's social function.

The Subjective Necessity—Social Work Values and Societal Values

What Addams called the "subjective necessity" referred, at least partially, to values. It has long been a generally accepted belief among social workers that their values are somehow qualitatively or quantitatively different from those of the rest of society. The 1958 Working Definition of Social Work Practice, sponsored by the National Association of Social Workers, listed unique values as one of the defining attributes of social work practice.[19] In her 1959 study of *The Teaching of Values and Ethics in Social Work Education*, one of the volumes in the Council on Social Work Education Curriculum Study, Muriel Pumphrey said, "Despite difficulties with precise definitions there seems to be little doubt in the minds of practitioners representing all the professional specialties that social workers together are working toward some commonly held notions of how they would like to see society organized and social living conducted."[20] Siporin, in a widely read introductory practice text, states, "Social workers have long been distinguished from other helping professionals by their explicit and distinctive value system. The philosophy base embodies the ideals and the faith of social workers and serves as an ideology. It is a central feature of social work as a normative discipline."[21] State social work licensing laws often recognize social work values. The Alabama law, for example, defines social work practice as, "The professional application of social work values, principles, and techniques . . ."[22] Marian Sanders, a lay critic of social work, once observed, ". . . the explicitness with which social workers practice what they preach tends to jolt those accustomed only to the more abstract manifestations of democracy."[23]

Although social work scholars contend that social work values are in some ways unique, when they seriously discuss the issue, most back off a bit and admit that social work values are not entirely independent of major societal values, but are really extensions of those values. However, as Abbott has written, "It is important to note . . . that social work's values historically have *not* been identical with those of the larger society."[24]

Just what are social work's values? Pike conducted a content analysis of the social work literature over the past twenty-five years, and extracted the following as the most commonly cited social work values:

- The inherent dignity and worth of the individual
- Society's responsibility for the individual's welfare
- Reciprocity between individuals and the society and the reciprocity between rights and responsibilities
- Client self-determination
- Individual potential for change[25]

Siporin asserts that the values most prized by social workers are altruism (a general value composed of love, caring, and social responsibility); belief in social independence and responsibility; concern for the poor and disadvantaged, and the deviant and dependent; dedication to justice and equality; and "socialized individualism in the sense of respect for inherent worth and individualized needs, for rights to socially responsible self-direction and self-realization."[26]

Although most social work theorists assert that social work values are unique and are in fact a defining characteristic of the profession, there are a few who disagree. Meinert, for example, has written,

> Deeply imbedded in the profession is the belief that institutionalized social work is based on a trinity of identifiable knowledge, values, and skills. Certainly a shared body of knowledge and skills exists in social work. [I] strongly [question], however, whether a system of values is truly present. [I argue] that values in social work are nonexistent; they are a myth, a myth we can live without. If social workers do possess any "values," they are not unique ones, but only preference patterns shared by the general population.[27]

Are social work values different from those of the general society, or is this simply a myth, as Meinert contends? There has been a good deal of research done on this question, and it indicates that social workers do indeed possess values different from those of comparison groups. In a 1958 study Kidneigh and Lundberg compared characteristics of students entering social work with those of students in six other professions, using data from the College Vocabulary Test and the Authoritarian

Personality Social Attitudes Battery. The social work students were found to be more liberal than other students in regard to antidemocratic tendencies, ethnocentrism, political-economic conservatism, and interpretation of traditional family ideology. The authors concluded, ". . . by self-selection, school selection, or a combination of these with other variables, the social work student group in this study demonstrated social attitudes that separated them significantly from students in the six other professions . . ."[28]

A number of studies have supported those of Kidneigh and Lundberg. Sharwell found that social work students were significantly different from the general population in their attitudes toward public dependency. Abbott looked at four value dimensions hypothesized to represent social work values and found that social work students scored significantly higher on each than did their peers enrolled in other professional curricula. McLeod and Meyer developed a list of ten attitude dimensions (individual worth versus system goals, etc.). They labeled one pole of each as the social work value and hypothesized that "social workers as a group are closer than the average of the rest of the population to the pole we state is the social work value." They compared social work graduate students with untrained social workers, and found significant differences on seven of the ten dimensions. They then compared M.S.W. social workers with teachers, and found significant differences on eight of the ten dimensions.[29]

Do people choose social work because they have values different from those of the greater society and view social work as a career compatible with their values? Or do they acquire social work values during professional socialization? The answer appears to be *both*. Kidneigh and Lundberg concluded that social work students came from a unique pool, that they were not selected from the same common pool as students in other professions. Abbott found that the values of beginning social work students were different from those of their peers in other professions. Sharwell found that beginning social work students differed significantly from the general population in their attitude toward public dependency. Research also shows that the values of social work students become even more different from those of the general population during the course of their education. Judah looked at the values of B.S.W. students and found that they changed between admission and graduation. Sharwell found the same in a study of M.S.W. students. Abbott concluded that professional social work education does have an important impact on students, especially in the area of value orientation. Merdinger states that the findings of her study "suggest that social work students were predisposed to certain values and professional positions and strengthened these stances during the course of their education."[30]

Conclusion

In her discussion of the subjective necessity for the social settlements, Addams stumbled upon the real basis of social work's dualistic nature, and her point is still valid. There is both an objective and a subjective necessity for social work in modern society. The objective necessity is society's need to manage the many problems of dependency and deviance in order to maintain social stability. This necessity leads to recognition of social work as a profession. This necessity (or purpose or function, if you will) is, like all professional functions, inherently conservative. However, there is also a subjective necessity for social work. This necessity is the motivation of individuals to pursue careers in social work. People attracted to social work are generally individuals who wish to operationalize a social conscience; they choose social work as their career for essentially moral reasons. Individually and collectively, they tend to be liberal, change-oriented, sometimes even radical. We therefore have a profession with a conservative mandate from society, but a liberal/radical mandate from its own members. The result is that there has always been and will always be a dynamic tension between the profession and society and a continued focus of dualisms.

What about Reamer's concern that people now enter social work because they view it as an attractive career, rather than a calling? Social work and social workers are not immune to the political swings of society. When society enters a conservative era, the subjective and the objective necessities move closer together—i.e., the motivations of people for entering social work more closely resemble the function assigned to the profession by the larger society. This was true in the late 1950s, when Marian Sanders referred to social work as "a profession chasing its tail" because she observed that practitioners were more concerned with psychotherapy and professional status than with helping the poor. Fifteen years later Harry Specht was predicting the "deprofessionalization of social work" because he believed the profession was overemphasizing activism—i.e., the subjective necessity was becoming dominant.[31] We now have Reamer sounding the alarm that the conception of social work as a career is eclipsing that of social work as a calling.

I conclude this essay with the observation that social work is both a calling *and* a career. The calling reflects the subjective necessity: the desire, at least by many people who choose social work, to operationalize a social conscience. The career reflects society's need to turn over a major problem area, in this case the management of dependency, to an organized occupation. When society is in a liberal phase, the subjective necessity for social work is emphasized. When society is in a conservative mood, the objective necessity dominates. The 1980s have been a decade of conservatism, a continuation of the '70s' "me generation," hence private practice, third-party reimbursement, and licensure have dominated. What the 1990s will be, we don't know. However, rest assured that the subjective necessity is now as it was a hundred years ago, a permanent feature of the profession.

Notes

1. Nina Toren, *Social Work: The Case of a Semi-Profession* (Beverly Hills, Calif.: Sage Publications, 1972), 19.

2. Clarke A. Chambers, "An Historical Perspective On Political Action vs. Individual Treatment," in *Current Issues in Social Work Seen in Historical Perspective* (New York: Council on Social Work Education, 1962), 56.

3. Joanna C. Colcord and Ruth Mann, eds., *Mary E. Richmond, The Long View: Papers and Addresses* (New York: Russell Sage Foundation, 1930).

4. Porter R. Lee, *Social Work as Cause and Function, and Other Papers* (New York: New York School of Social Work, 1937), 4–9.

5. Eveline M. Burns, "Social Welfare Is Our Commitment," *The*

Social Welfare Forum, 1958 (New York: Columbia University Press, 1958), 4–5.

6. William Schwartz, "Small Group Science and Group Work Practice," *Social Work* 8 (October 1963):40–1.

7. Roy Lubove, "Social Work and the Life of the Poor," *The Nation* (23 May 1966):609–611. Charles Frankel, "Obstacles to Action for Human Welfare," *The Social Welfare Forum, 1961* (New York: Columbia University Press, 1961), 281. Neil Gilbert and Harry Specht, "The Incomplete Profession," *Social Work* 19 (November 1974):665–74.

8. Ralph Pumphrey, "Compassion and Protection: Dual Motivations in Social Welfare," *Social Service Review* 23 (1959):21–29.

9. Jane Addams, *Twenty Years at Hull House* (New York: Macmillan, 1916), 125.

10. Christopher Lasch, *The New Radicalism in America 1889–1963—The Intellectual As A Social Type* (New York: Vintage Books, 1965), 11.

11. Philip R. Popple, "The Social Work Profession: A Reconceptualization," *Social Service Review* 59 (1985):560–77.

12. Abraham Flexner, "Is Social Work a Profession?" in *Proceedings of the National Conference of Charities and Correction, 1915* (Chicago: Hildmann Printing Co., 1915), 576–90. Ernest Greenwood, "Attributes of a Profession," *Social Work* 2 (July, 1957):44–55.

13. Max Weber, *Economy and Society* (Totowa, N.J.: Bedminster Press, 1968).

14. John B. Cullen, *The Structure of Professionalism—A Quantitative Examination* (New York: Petrocelli Books, 1978), 8.

15. H. Jamous and B. Peloille, "Professions or Self-Perpetuating Systems? Changes in the French University Hospital System," in J.A. Jackson, *Professions and Professionalization* (Cambridge: Cambridge University Press, 1970), 111.

16. Charles Atherton, "The Social Assignment of Social Work," *Social Service Review* 43 (1969): 421–29. Charles Cowger and Charles Atherton, "Social Control: A Rationale for Social Welfare," *Social Work* 19 (July 1974):456–62.

17. Atherton, "The Social Assignment" 421.

18. Ibid., 425.

19. Harriet M. Bartlett, "Toward Clarification and Improvement of Social Work Practice," *Social Work* 3 (April 1958):3–9.

20. Muriel W. Pumphrey, *The Teaching of Values and Ethics in Social Work Education* (New York: Council on Social Work Education, 1959), 11.

21. Max Siporin, *Introduction To Social Work Practice* (New York: Macmillan, 1975), 61.

22. Code of Alabama 1975, S34-30—S34-30-58, p. 1.

23. Marian K. Sanders, "Social Work: A Profession Chasing Its Tail," *Harper's Magazine* (March 1957):59.

24. Ann A. Abbott, *Professional Choices: Values at Work* (Silver Spring, Md: NASW, 1988), 32.

25. Cathy Pike, "Values and Social Work: An Inquiry," (Tuscaloosa, Ala.: Unpublished paper, 1986), 9.

26. Max Siporin, "Moral Philosophy in Social Work Today," *Social Service Review* 56 (1982): 518.

27. Roland G. Meinert, "Values in Social Work Called Dysfunctional Myth," *Journal of Social Welfare* 6 (Spring 1980):5.

28. John C. Kidneigh and Horace W. Lundberg, "Are Social Work Students Different?" *Social Work* 3 (July 1958):60.

29. George R. Sharwell, "Can Values Be Taught? A Study of Two Variables Related to Orientation of Social Work Graduate Students Toward Public Dependency," *Journal of Education for Social Work* 10 (Spring 1974):99–105. Abbott, *Professional Choices,* 107–108. Donna L. McLeod and Henry J. Meyer, "A Study of the Values of Social Workers," in Edwin J. Thomas, ed., *Behavioral Science for Social Workers* (New York: The Free Press, 1967), 401–416.

30. Kidneigh and Lundberg, "Are Social Work Students Different?" 60–61. Abbott, *Professional Choices,* 59–60, 107–108. Sharwell, "Can Values Be Taught?" 99–105. E. H. Judah, "Values: The Uncertain Component in Social Work," *Journal of Education for Social Work* 15 (Spring 1979):79–86. J. M. Merdinger, "Socialization into a Profession: The Case of Undergraduate Social Work Students," *Journal of Education for Social Work* 18 (1982) 2:12–19.

31. Marian Sanders, "Social Work: A Profession Chasing Its Tail." Harry Specht, "The Deprofessionalization of Social Work," *Social Work* 17 (March 1972):3–15.

CHAPTER NINE

Moral Goodness and Black Women: Late Nineteenth Century Community Caregivers

Wilma Peebles-Wilkins and Beverly Koerin

The moral purposes of social work are best understood in the context of the sense of social obligation or responsibility which developed within a profession evolving during the late nineteenth and early twentieth centuries—a period of social reform in American society. The religious traditions noted by Siporin and the sense of obligation which characterized the social intervention of that era found a similar expression in segregated black communities before the development of a more universal social service delivery system. As noted by Reamer, early social work focused on "improving the morals of paupers"; similarly, in the black community, the early community caregivers initially focused on the individual behavior of other black persons. These developments in black communities and the moral commitments driving the collective expression grew out of a common heritage and common bond of slavery, segregation, and oppression.

The historical evolution of professional training for social workers, which grew out of volunteer charity work in the dominant culture, is well documented and frequently cited. However, during the same period, between 1896 and 1915, foundations were also laid for the professional training of black social workers.[1] Social service practices developed historically in a dual racial sphere, and developments in local black communities paralleled reform in the dominant culture.[2] Black women provided a range of caregiving services not totally dissimilar from those offered by the friendly visitors of the Charity Organization Society and the workers of the Settlement House Movement.

The caregiving mission emanating from what Siporin has termed the "social ethic of mutual aid" raises a number of issues about contemporary social work practices, and the relationship of these practices to social work heritage in general and to that heritage within the black community in particular. Siporin's[3] moral philosophy arguments raise thought-provoking questions about the profession's contemporary role and the assignment of professional social workers in relation to the collective good. These are fundamental questions to which there are no simple answers—question about the "proper allocation of resources, about political values and about social justice,"[4] questions about the role of social workers in community-oriented services and in the collaborative efforts with informal caregivers, questions about "those aspects [of our work] which have to do with the care of one another in society and the organization of that care,"[5] and especially questions about the role of professional social work in supporting or undermining the unique heritage of caregiving in the black community.

Specific focus on the collective expression of black foremothers and forefathers enriches our knowledge of the moral convictions which form the historical and contemporary context of caregiving. Black women community caregivers ("charity workers") provided a range of social service programs to the black community. Biographical, autobiographical, and related descriptive accounts help us retrieve and understand these activities, and the philosophy and zeal which characterized the mission of caregiving in the segregated black community prior to the development of more universal social service programs. As described by Reid and Popple in the introduction, these descriptive accounts shed light on "ways of life and rules of conduct" or the "moral philosophy" underpinning these pioneering efforts in the black community.

Influences on the Late Nineteenth Century World View

The moral philosophy and world view of late nineteenth- and early twentieth-century black women caregivers developed in the contexts of black heritage, racial oppression and segregation, developing social changes, and the changing roles of women which were emerging.

Major transformations occurred as a result of social processes and social movements: Urbanization, industrialization, immigration, political democratization, evangelicalism. These social forces contributed to both the development of social welfare and the role of women as agents of social welfare. The urban-industrial society of this era was viewed as a dangerous and chaotic environment, which was rapidly generating new social problems. Public and private social welfare programs and organizations developed in response to these problems, as a means of addressing both the unmet needs of individuals and families, and society's unmet need for social order in the face of massive social change. During the social reform of the late nineteenth century, professional social work emerged as American women, for the first time, assumed a greater role outside the home as volunteer community caregivers.

With the increasing separation of home from workplace and the related segregation of work and family roles, a side effect of urban-industrial economic development, the home was idealized as a refuge or retreat from the unsettling external world. Women, as keepers of the domestic retreat, became the symbolic stabilizing link between the passing agrarian culture and the emerging urban-industrial social order. The role of women as symbolic protectors of the traditional moral order was expressed in the image of the Victorian woman and the "cults" of "true womanhood" and "virtuous womanhood."[6] These "cults" or images of women, emphasized the virtues of purity, piety, and domesticity,[7] and idealized woman as "the repository of special sensibility and refinement."[8] These "inherent" traits made women "uniquely suited to the mission of alleviation and uplift," in that women "possessed those qualities of character—steeped . . . in Christian love—that prepared them for lives of service to others."[9]

Many of the activities of nineteenth-century women reformers were characterized by a "missionary zeal" reflecting the religious roots or auspices of the movements in which these women were involved—e.g., the abolition and temperance movements. In these social reform movements, women acted in the context of their "proper place" in society, engaging in church and community efforts to protect the purity of the home and the morality of society. Yet, the women's rights movement also grew out of these activities. As women began to organize these moral crusades, they became increasingly aware of the disadvantages they experienced by virtue of their confinement to the domestic sphere, of the limitations on the acceptability of their public roles, and of discrimination in the workplace which hampered the ability of lower-income women to provide for their families.

The history of women in social reform, social welfare, and women's rights activities is largely written as a history of nineteenth-century upper- and middle-class white women. Yet, black women were also involved in organizing for social betterment, and were "moral agents" of the black community. The organization of black women for moral purposes also led to the development of community caregiving and social service activities. Concern for morality, a sense of religious duty, and a desire to help their fellow humans formed the basis for all forms of social care in both the black and white communities of the nineteenth century.

Leiby described the religious fervor which characterized the nineteenth-century view of life. He noted that, "Religious ideas were the most important intellectual influence on American welfare institutions in the nineteenth century. People interested in charity and corrections usually professed a religious motive and claimed a religious sanction. Clergymen were prominent in both administration and reform."[10] According to Leiby, these religious ideas were transformed into secular ideas about social welfare in the late nineteenth century. In addition to religious ideas, the humanistic orientation in the foundation of professional caregiving stemmed from attitudes about charity and ideas about social well-being; from other forms of social thought rooted in Judeo-Christian altruism; from benevolent attitudes expressed in the writings of Graeco-Roman scholars such as Seneca and other pre-Christian Western influences; and, for the black community, from the West African cultural emphasis on the collective good. Expansion of the social work knowledge and skills base during this period offered an opportunity for further development of social welfare or formal caregiving, with a social justice emphasis. However, similar community caregiving persisted on an informal basis and flourished in the black community through mutual help and voluntary organizations.

Caregiving in the Black Community

During the late nineteenth- and early twentieth-century reform period in social welfare history, American society was segregated, and blacks for the most part were excluded from the mainstream progressive movement.[11] Many black people lived in the South and were victims of the sharecropper system, lynching, and other forms of harassment. Blacks who migrated to northern cities seeking factory work often experienced employment discrimination. Overall, the black population was outside the mainstream of social reform which benefited white citizens in the North. Because of these demographic and social factors and the persistence of racist ideology, many in the dominant society were concerned about the ability of blacks to be successful and responsible citizens,[12] and questioned the basic morality of blacks in general. Documentation in social welfare history reflects these negative attitudes associated with social segregation. However, relatively little attention has been paid to the strengths of the black community reflected in patterns of community caregiving. Focus on the collective expression of the black community, and particularly of black women, enriches our understanding of the moral convictions which form the social context of contemporary caregiving. Mutual aid activities persisted in segregated communities, though they were not part of formal mainstream structures.

Some historians have attributed late nineteenth- and early twentieth-century organizational developments among black women to the influence of black leader Booker T. Washington, who advised black Americans to use self-help and mutual aid as survival techniques,[13] or to the broader influence of the nineteenth-century book *Self-help*, by the British doctor, Samuel Smiles, which widely influenced the development of friendly societies and credit union–type activities.[14] However, the foundations of self-help and mutual-aid activities among black women were laid much earlier. Peer and social support activities—such as child care, midwifery, health care for sick children, and group socialization of children—are described in accounts of the activities of black women in slave networks as far back as the colonial period.[15] More formal origins of social convictions about mutual help in the black community can be documented during the period between the Revolutionary War and the Civil War. To date, the most well-known black mutual aid organization is the Free African Society founded in Philadelphia in 1787 by Absalom Jones and clergyman Richard Allen. This church-related model of influence recurs throughout the historical evolution of black organizations in America.[16]

After the Civil War and into the early twentieth century, church and mutual aid organizations, oriented toward social and spiritual betterment and community education, were formed in the black community. Financial and "mental" resources were pooled to provide rehabilitative and developmental social welfare programs. There were social and economic development programs and efforts to help delinquents and victims of poverty; at the same time educational guidance and nurturance were fostered through early intervention programs, such as child care and other youth-oriented activities designed to mold good character. This focus was similar to the "moral and spiritual uplift" orientation of mainstream early American social work organizations such as the Charity Organization Society.

Characteristic of the social climate of the time, leaders in the black community viewed high morals and good character as keys to success. Even in their earlier history, blacks believed that a special calling or divine command inspired the personal sacrifices and mutual aid activities of such women as Harriet Tubman.[17] While all these activities were designed to promote freedom and social justice for the group, these human rights interests were very American concepts with implications for the treatment of the whole society. Additionally, black leaders, male and female, were concerned about social betterment and the good of the group in all aspects of life. The family ethic and the work ethic permeated this "group good" orientation. This conformity to the work and family ethic, also prevalent in the dominant society, was religious in its orientation, and, as Abramovitz notes, persists in contemporary secular social welfare policies and practices.[18] As informal caregiving in

American communities was partially replaced in the late nineteenth and early twentieth centuries by institutionalized social
welfare programs, other forms of caregiving continued in the
black community through voluntary associations and, in particular, through the church as a primary institution of black
culture.[19]

> The religious experience was a group heritage and a creative
> personal impetus. At once secular and holy, a religious senti-
> ment suffused black thought and generated a dynamic for
> black action. . . . eternal membership in the Kingdom of God
> made secular ideals sacred. Both served as bases for social
> criticism and earthly hope. Although such commitments and
> aspirations were the same for the scores of whites, they had
> a special meaning for black Americans.[20]

This religious expression took the form of social obligations
which represented the principles and values of a Judeo-Christian heritage. By the same token, the black cultural sense of
social obligations also represented a transformation of the West
African tradition which emphasized the collective good, as opposed to the Western focus on the individual. This transformed
sense of social obligation and concern for the "group good" is
believed by some to have permeated the culture of the black
community, and is sometimes referred to as *a helping tradition*.[21]

Black women were central to the helping tradition of the
black community through their roles in the "natural helping
networks" of extended family and fictive kin relations,[22] and
through their roles in the church. In describing this cultural
expression and function of black women, Loewenberg and Bogin
stated that "religion was pivotal to black American life," and
"womanhood in each of its phases was sanctioned by religious
values."[23] Other historians such as Neverdon-Morton have documented the "social uplift" orientation of black women activists who provided a range of educational, health, and welfare
services in southern communities between 1895 and 1925. Similar to other nineteenth-century women reformers, they worked
with a "missionary zeal"—the term used by Neverdon-Morton
to describe the social justice and related caregiving activities

among black women within the framework of the then-existing black culture.[24]

Hine (1986) states, in relation to the black existence in the late nineteenth century:

> . . . America moved inexorably toward a society best charac-
> terized as "biracial dualism". While white Americans, north
> and south, accepted black subordination as representing the
> Darwinian natural order, black leaders of the race focused
> almost completely on winning educational, political, and eco-
> nomic rights. Black women, on the other hand, focused on
> eradicating negative images of their sexuality. Thus, by the
> late 1890's there developed a major division of emphasis
> within the black protest tradition. Black men attacked racial
> discrimination as it operated in the public corridors of power.
> Black women, whose center of influence had always existed
> primarily in the family, in the church, and in their female
> associations, believed that part of the overall struggle for true
> racial advancement depended upon the extent to which they
> obliterated all negative sexual images of themselves.[25]

Black Women as Moral Agents and Caregivers

Black women leaders were particularly concerned about negative characterizations of black women. Unlike white women
involved in voluntary associations and social reform movements, black women had to *prove* their moral goodness to the
dominant society which accepted white women's inherent role
as "moral agents." Social attitudes about black people in general, and black women in particular, help to explain the over-
tones of social control resounding from the black leadership
class. However, the late nineteenth-century *race women's* ambitious call for stronger moral standards was not at variance
with the larger society's focus on helping.

The mission of black women initially focused on moral
uplift associated with individual sexual behavior. This mission
later included social reform activities characteristic of the period, as black women began to participate in caregiving and
social service activities. During this time, black women were
"singled out and advertised" as having lower sexual standards
than other women.[26] Fannie B. Williams, a black school teacher

162

in the South but born in the North, observed that slavery had made the black woman "the only woman in America for whom virtue was not an ornament and a necessity" because of her vulnerability to sexual abuse under slavery.[27]

Negative images of black women undermined and stereo-typed all black women. "Race women," such as Josephine St. Pierre Ruffin, stood for "purity and mental worth" and made special efforts to refute negative claims by projecting positive images and explaining negative behaviors associated with lack of education and with social and economic oppression. White women, as they began to organize women's rights and moral crusade organizations, often excluded black women. Josephine St. Pierre Ruffin asserted, in her address to the First National Conference of Colored Women in 1895, that southern white women had protested the admission of colored women into any national organization, based on perceptions of their immorality. She advocated for the association of black women, a means of counteracting these views: "Now with an army of organized women, standing for purity and mental worth, we in ourselves deny the charge and open the eyes of the world to a state of affairs to which they have been blind, often willfully so . . ."[28] In her 1926 article on "The Virginia Industrial School," Janie Porter Barrett described the role of the National Association of Colored Women's Clubs in refuting a remark made by an American white man "who declared from a public platform in London that there was not a decent colored woman in all America."[29] Reactions to such negative comments about the black American woman were described as "the libel that united a race."[30] Barrett says about this united front:

> No time was lost in denying what this white man had said, but the women accepted the challenge and the National Asso-ciation was organized for the purpose of cooperating with all colored women to raise to a higher plane their homes and their moral and civil life. They took as their motto, "Lifting As We Climb," and that small group of women representing a few states started out to reach every Negro woman in America.[31]

Mutual aid networks in the black community were often gender-based membership groups. Groups comprised of black women began to develop only during the pre-Civil War period, but black women's clubs, nationally federated in 1896, existed in local communities during the 1830s.[32] Black women made many contributions through leadership roles in these gender-based voluntary associations. However, their social service contributions are usually excluded from historical analyses of the development of social welfare and social work.

Operating out of churches and educational facilities, southern black women in Alabama, Florida, Georgia, Maryland, North Carolina, Tennessee, and Virginia provided services within the social institutions of family, religion, and education. Community action programs and well-developed "human communication networks"[33] for providing social services were developed. A few examples include Janie Porter Barrett's Locust Street Settlement in Virginia; the Mt. Meigs Reformatory for Juvenile Negro Law-Breakers, founded in Alabama under the leadership of Mrs. Booker T. Washington; Carrie Steele's orphanage in Georgia; Millie E. Hale's hospital in Tennessee; Eartha White's services for the homeless in Florida in 1928; Charlotte Hawkins Brown's school for girls in North Carolina; and the St. Frances Orphan Asylum and Academy for Colored Girls, founded by the Oblate Sisters of Providence, a Catholic religious order for black women in Maryland.

The volunteer services performed by these black women stemmed in part from their sense of Christian altruism, and in part from their African heritage which had not been destroyed by enslavement. During the early stages of development, these black women caregivers described themselves as "race women." "Race women" had broad-based racial goals, cared for disadvantaged blacks, and confronted the social oppression which made black men and women victimized and powerless. When speaking before a 1910 New York City meeting of the Charity Organization Society, Mary Church Terrell, a noted figure in the black women's movement, described the goal of "race women" as "regenerating and elevating" the race.[34] "Race women" represented educated and affluent black society, and to a great extent perceived themselves as role models of morality for those in the black community who were victims of oppression. In rural communities, for example, black women were expected to keep themselves "straight and strong" to improve the overall quality of life in these isolated spots.[35] Like the charity workers and the settlement house workers, the black women volunteers operating in a segregated society were motivated by religious faith. Just as the charity workers saw poverty as a sign of bad habits and moral failings, "race women" of the period believed that "ignorance and immorality" led to poverty.

Education was emphasized as the major force for improving the overall quality of life for blacks. During this period black women worked either as teachers or as domestics. The many schools and educational programs developed by black women added to the liberal arts curriculum a focus on domestic science and domestic arts. The domestic training aspect of the curriculum was pragmatic and helped young black women find jobs. However, the domestic science focus in the curriculum also prepared young black women for home life. Much of the philosophical orientation of black club women placed a great emphasis on the moral uplift of black women. They believed that lack of knowledge about home life made black women "social and moral liabilities."[36]

An examination of the lives and world view of selected black women leaders in voluntary associations enriches our understanding of how moral commitments translated into collective expressions of social conviction. Over time, the sense of religious and moral obligations which emanated from their convictions were secularized. Highlights of the views of selected black women leaders prominent during the period will offer greater insight into the transformation of religious and moral views to more secular attitudes. Mary Church Terrell is one of the most notable women for the period under discussion.

The Influence of Mary Church Terrell

Mary Church Terrell (1863–1954) is a significant figure in the history of voluntary associations in black communities, in the history of social work and social welfare, and in the national and international study of human rights. Educated at Oberlin College in the "gentlemen's curriculum," she came from a well-to-do black family and was very fair-skinned. However, she was also very clear about her racial identity, and committed herself to improving the quality of life for other blacks whose opportunities were restricted by societal oppression. Her life's work and social activism span several significant eras of social changes in race relations and civil rights for both women and blacks in America.[37] Though she rarely appears in standard social welfare historical accounts, Mary Church Terrell's life work has been highlighted in social and women's history. Although the sit-in as a technique is associated with 1960s college student activism at lunch counters in Greensboro, North Carolina, Mary Church Terrell was the "regulator and mother of the sit-in" technique.[38] During the 1950s she used this technique to lead groups of protesters against segregation at lunch counters and cafeterias in the District of Columbia. In other areas of domestic and international human rights, she lectured on women's suffrage and against the lynching of black men in the United States. In addition to her volunteer work for racial uplift in the black community, she worked in cooperation with outstanding historical figures such as Jane Addams.

Unlike the problems of omission or lack of documentation associated with black history, the circumstances surrounding the life of Mary Church Terrell are well documented in both primary and secondary source material, in part because Mary Church Terrell was herself a prolific writer. While there is a need for greater documentation of the historical contributions of black women, outstanding scholarship already exists to describe the organizations that African-American women created in the late nineteenth and early twentieth centuries.[39] Terrell's writings and the activities of the black women's club movement in America offer considerable insight into the philosophical orientation and world view underlying the community caregiving activities of these associations. Her articles about club work among black women provide an overview of the directives issued to the membership of the National Association of Colored Women under Terrell's leadership.

Mary Church Terrell was the first president of the National Association of Colored Women, which was organized in 1896. The extent and strength of her influence on the organization and on black women across the country is symbolized by the fact that, after serving as president for five years, she was awarded the distinction of an honorary lifetime presidency. Her descriptions of the organization's purpose, the role of black women, and the need for racial uplift are articulated in her many writings. Her scholarship is imbued with an emphasis on the family ethic, the work ethic, and moral and social obligation.[40]

Enthusiasm and zeal were reflected in early club efforts to improve the unhealthy living conditions of the nineteenth-century poor. Terrell took the following stance on housing conditions: "Against the one-room cabin we have inaugurated a vigorous crusade. When families of eight or ten men, women and children are all huddled promiscuously together in a single apartment, a condition common among our poor all over the land, there is little hope of inculcating morality and modesty."[41]

The goals of club women also reflected their interest in child development, stemming from mid-nineteenth-century attitudinal changes and broader social concerns about the well-being of children. Efforts to combat delinquency led to the development of preventive, substitute, and supportive child welfare services. Based on the belief that "crime [was] conceived in thought before it [was] executed in deed," black women were encouraged to create community programs to help black youths assume responsibility for their thoughts and learn to control them.[42] The "duties" and "obligations" of black club women were then conceived in terms of preventing and responding to juvenile delinquency, providing better educational instruction for children, establishing day care and early childhood education programs, introducing into the black community parent education programs modeled after the Mother's Congress, and focusing on adult role modeling for young children to avoid the formation of "evil habits" which even "Christianizing" could not eliminate.[43]

All these ideas were associated with supporting working mothers and strengthening the family unit through systematic and organized community planning. The strength of this family focus is reflected in remarks such as one made by Terrell in a 1901 speech describing the duties of black club women: "Homes, more homes, better homes, purer homes, is the text upon which our sermons have been and will be preached."[44] Although the importance of home life was always stressed and the role of black women in relation to home and family emphasized, there was also a pragmatic recognition of the impact of economic oppression and the need for mothers to work. The response to financial need was one of support, rather than disapproval or blaming the victim. Terrell, like Florence Kelley and Jane Addams, believed that the community was responsible for developing supportive child welfare services and services for working mothers.

Black club women were very concerned about the treatment of the children of working mothers left in substitute child care arrangements. One of Terrell's most graphic examples described a fourteen-month-old infant left in a boarding home by his mother while she worked. The hands and legs of the infant were deformed from rheumatism caused by being left to sleep in an unheated room during the winter. Establishment of day nurseries was viewed as one of the "greatest services possible to humanity and to the race."[45]

The goals and objectives of improving home life by supporting working mothers and making quality child care more readily available were sometimes difficult to accomplish because of limited funds. In some communities the public schools had started kindergarten programs, and in other communities kindergartens and day nurseries were organized as part of black settlement houses and community centers. However, some communities were unable to accumulate enough money to fulfill club objectives. In such communities Terrell advised affluent club members to open their homes to the children of working mothers.

From the social welfare perspective, these altruistic mandates to black club women led not only to the provision of developmental and rehabilitative social welfare programs, but also to progress in social controls. Terrell, viewing the negative behavior of some black women as a barrier to racial progress and success, wrote, ". . . if the call of duty were disregarded altogether, policy and self-preservation would demand that we go down among the lowly, the illiterate, and even the vicious to whom we are bound by the ties of race and sex, and put forth every possible effort to uplift and reclaim them."[46] The social control efforts of volunteers from the Charity Organization Society and the Settlement House Movement have been noted by historians. Trattner suggests that "purposeful planning" and some limitations on individual freedom were the only means of achieving "justice and social cohesion" when helping those in stressful life circumstances.[47] Mary Church Terrell's moral prescriptions to black club women certainly seem to fit the pattern of the dominant society, but race made the social control more complex.

Conclusion

Through their united efforts, black women, like their white sisters, assumed important roles in community caregiving and in the development of social service programs to promote racial advancement. Initially religiously motivated, their mission focused on both individual behavioral expectations and progressive social reforms. This sense of "duty to the race" became secularized in health care, social settlements, child care, and other services provided in segregated communities and was later, for the most part, absorbed by universal social service provisions.

While this discussion has focused on the moral mission of selective community care provisions in historically segregated black communities, the sense of duty emanating from these mutual aid networks and voluntary associations has implications for contemporary intervention. This historical dimension is particularly germane to contemporary community service delivery patterns which require the creative use of resource systems, mutual aid groups, and other types of informal help. The secular obligations of the social work profession evolved from a tradition of moral, value, and ethical commitment to society which should be revitalized. As part of this revitalization, long-standing mutual aid traditions in the black community should be acknowledged, recognized, and considered in the contemporary context of social intervention.

Notes

The authors wish to thank Professor Barbara Risman, Coordinator of the Women's Studies Minor, North Carolina State University, for her review and thoughtful comments.

1. Edyth L. Ross, *Black Heritage in Social Welfare* (Metuchen, N.J.: The Scarecrow Press, 1978), 422–23.

2. Dolores G. Norton et. al., *The Dual Perspective* (Washington, D.C.: Council on Social Work Education, 1978), 3–7.

3. Max Siporin, "Moral Philosophy in Social Work," *Social Service Review* 56 (1982): 518–31.

4. Tony Byrne and Colin F. Padfield, *Social Services Made Simple* (London: William Hienemann, 1987).

5. Nelson Reid and Wilma Peebles-Wilkins, "Social Work and the Liberal Arts: An Essay on Renewing the Commitment," *Journal of Social Work Education* 27 (1991) 2: 217.

6. See, e.g., Nancy F. Cott, *The Bonds of Womanhood: "Woman's Sphere" in New England, 1780–1835* (New Haven: Yale University Press, 1977). Barbara Welter, "The Cult of True Womanhood: 1820–1860" in Michael Gordon, ed., *The American Family in Socio-Historical Perspective*, 2nd ed. (New York: St. Martin's Press, 1978). Sheila M. Rothman, *Woman's Proper Place: A History of Changing Ideals and Practices, 1870 to the Present* (New York: Basic Books, 1978).

7. Barbara Welter. "The Cult," 313.

8. Sheila M. Rothman, *Woman's Proper Place*, 22–23.

9. Clarke A. Chambers, "Women in the Creation of the Profession of Social Work," *Social Service Review* 60 (1986):4.

10. James Leiby, *A History of Social Welfare and Social Work in the United States* (New York: Columbia University Press, 1978), 12.

11. Cynthia Neverdon-Morton, *Afro-American Women of the South and the Advancement of the Race, 1895–1925* (Knoxville: The University of Tennessee Press, 1989), 9.

12. June Axinn and Herman Levin, *Social Welfare: A History of the American Response to Need* (New York: Harper & Row, 1975), 120, 175.

13. Ross, *Black Heritage*, 192.

14. Byrne and Padfield, *Social Services Made Simple*, 8.

15. Deborah White, "Female Slaves: Sex Roles and Status in the Antebellum Plantation South," *Journal of Family History* (Fall 1983), 248–61.

16. See, e.g., Ira Berlin, *Slaves Without Masters: The Free Negro in the Antebellum South* (New York: Pantheon Books, 1974). King E. Davis, "Black Fund-Raising" (Unpublished Ph.D. dissertation, Brandeis University, 1972), 335–38. Gary B. Nash, *Forging Freedom: The Formation of Philadelphia's Black Community, 1720–1840* (Cambridge, Mass.: Harvard University Press, 1988). Debra Newman, "Black

Women in the Era of the American Revolution in Pennsylvania," *Journal of Negro History* (July 1976): 276–89. Linda Perkins "Black Women in Racial 'Uplift' Prior to Emancipation," in Filomina Steady, ed., *The Black Woman Cross-Culturally* (Cambridge, Mass.: Schenkman Publishing Company, 1981), 317–348. Ross, *Black Heritage*, 29–35.

17. Paula Giddings, *When and Where I Enter* (New York: William Morrow, 1984), 102. John Hope Franklin, *From Slavery to Freedom: A History of Negro Americans* (New York: Random House, 1971), 482. Cynthia Neverdon-Morton, *Afro-American Women of the South and the Advancement of the Race, 1895–1925* (Knoxville: The University of Tennessee Press, 1989), 11.

18. Mimi Abramovitz, *Regulating the Lives of Women* (Boston: South End Press, 1988).

19. Darlene Clark Hine, "Lifting the Veil, Shattering the Silence: Black Women's History in Slavery and Freedom," in Hine, ed., *The State of Afro-American History*, (Baton Rouge: Louisiana State University Press, 1986), 223–49. Joanne M. Martin and Elmer P. Martin, *The Helping Tradition in the Black Family and Community* (Silver Spring, Md.: NASW, 1985). Wilma Peebles-Wilkins, "Black Women and American Social Welfare," *Affilia* 4 (Spring 1989): 33–44.

20. Bert James Loewenberg and Ruth Bogin, *Black Women in Nineteenth Century Life* (University Park: Pennsylvania State University Press, 1976), 9.

21. See, e.g., Herbert Gutman, *The Black Family in Slavery and Freedom, 1750–1925* (New York: Vintage Books, 1978). Martin and Martin, *The Helping Tradition* (Silver Spring, Md.: NASW, 1985).

22. Martin and Martin, *The Helping Tradition*, 37.

23. Loewenberg and Bogin, *Black Women*, 9.

24. Neverdon-Morton, *Afro-American Women*, 7.

25. Hine, "Lifting the Veil," 234.

26. Elise Johnson McDougald, "The Double Task: The Struggle of Negro Women for Sex and Race Emancipation," *Survey Graphics* (March 1925): 689–91.

27. Fannie B. Williams, "A Northern Negro's Autobiography," *The Independent* 57 (July 1904), 96, in Gerda Lerner, ed., *Black Women in White America*, (New York: Vintage Books, 1973), 165.

28. Josephine St. Pierre Ruffin, address at First National Conference of Colored Women, Boston, 1985, *The Women's Era* 2 (September 1985), 14, in Lerner, *Black Women in White America*, 442.

29. Janie Porter Barrett, "The Virginia Industrial School," *Southern Workman* 55 (August 1926): 353.

30. "Women Self-Reliant," *Women's Voice*, in Mary Church Ter-

rell Papers (Washington, D.C.: Moorland-Spingarn Research Center, Howard University, 1939).

31. Barrett, "The Virginia Industrial School," 353.

32. See, e.g., Lerner, *Black Women in White America*. Martin and Martin, *The Helping Tradition*, Newman, "Black Women in the Era."

33. Neverdon-Morton, *Afro-American Women*, 104.

34. Ibid., 3.

35. Ibid., 5.

36. Giddings, *When and Where*, 99–102.

37. Dorothy Sterling, *Black Foremothers: Three Lives* (New York: The Feminist Press, 1988).

38. Sylvia Render, "Afro-American Women: The Outstanding and the Obscure," *The Quarterly Journal of the Library of Congress* 32 (October 1975), 310.

39. See, e.g., Marilyn Dell Brady, "Organizing Afro-American Girls' Clubs in Kansas in the 1920's," *Frontiers*, 9 (1987) 2. Hine, "Lifting the Veil."

40. See, e.g., Beverly Washington Jones, "The Women's Club Movement," in Darlene Clark Hine, ed., *Quest for Equality: The Life and Writings of Mary Eliza Church Terrell, 1863–1954*, Vol. 13, *Black Women in United States History* (Brooklyn, N.Y.: Carlson Publishing, 1990), 17–29.

41. Mary Church Terrell, "Club Work of Colored Women," *Southern Workman* 30 (August 1901), 435–38, in Mary Church Terrell Papers. (Washington, D.C.: Moorland-Spingarn Research Center, Howard University), 436.

42. Mary Church Terrell, "The Duty of the National Association of Colored Women to the Race," *Church Review* (ca. 1899), 340–54. In Mary Church Terrell Papers, 345.

43. Terrell, "Club Work," 438.

44. Ibid., 437.

45. Terrell, "The Duty of the National Association of Colored Women," 344.

46. Ibid., 347.

47. Walter Trattner, *From Poor Law to Welfare State*, 4th ed. (New York: The Free Press, 1989), 160.

CHAPTER TEN

Responding to the Call

Maria O'Neil McMahon

Introduction: The Call to Serve the Poor

Is social work a career or a calling? In social work programs across the country today, social work is described primarily as "a profession." Although it is one of the least understood or appreciated professions, social work has the essential, identifiable characteristics of any profession, namely values, knowledge, method, purpose, and sanction.[1] As stated in earlier chapters, recently the values that characterized social work in the past have been questioned and challenged. The motives, beliefs, and behaviors of social workers are contrasted with the historically articulated values of the profession. A recalling and restating of the values and purpose of social work are needed.

Traditionally, social workers were identified with altruism, social justice, and public welfare. Gradually many social workers moved from working with the poor in local communities or public agencies to working with more affluent populations in such clinical areas as mental health and family therapy. As suggested by Walz, this shift in focus may have resulted from the rise of the middle class after World War II, which brought an increase in the number of both social workers and their clients, who came from more affluent populations. New generations of social workers and clients are socialized in a class in which secular, consumer-ethic white-collar influences prevail. The obvious shift in the profession from focusing on " the poor" to focusing on "the family" may not be a coincidence. The majority of clients of social work professionals today are middle-class people who seek out services and are willing to pay for them.[2]

Although middle-class clients may be easily served by other professionals, social workers have historically been the only source of help and advocacy for the materially poor. The need of the poor for advocates with institutional connections continues to prevail in American society. Recent studies indicate that the poorest age group in America is its most vulnerable group—children. There are over thirteen million children living in poverty in the United States today. Torrey and Rein reported in 1988 on the findings of their study in which they compared child poverty in the United States with child poverty in eight other affluent countries. The level of child poverty in the United States (17.1 percent) was the highest of all eight countries.[3] Who will speak out and advocate for the poor today? Social work practitioners and educators, agencies and educational programs, must address this question.

The profession of social work publicly expressed its recommitment to serving the poor in its *Code of Ethics*, passed by the Delegate Assembly in 1979 and implemented in July 1980. Two of the principles in Section VI of "The Social Workers Ethical Responsibility to Science" are

- The Social Worker should act to expand choice and opportunity for all persons, with special regard for disadvantaged or oppressed groups or persons.
- The social worker should advocate changes in policy and legislation to improve social conditions and to promote social justice.[4]

Because of the continued needs of the poor for equal opportunity, improved social conditions, and social justice, and because of the unique, documented commitment of the profession, there is strong reason for social workers to accept their ethical responsibility and respond to the call to serve the poor today. Seeing their career as a calling helps social workers find diverse and relevant ways to demonstrate their purpose, regardless of their degrees, their jobs, or their geographic locations.

The curriculum currently offered in professional social work education at both the B.S.W. and M.S.W. levels is a key area in need of attention. Are faculty and field instructors providing students with the teaching, modeling, and experience necessary for them to grow in understanding the meaning of such terms as "the poor," "social rights," "social development," "victimization," "public welfare," and "empowerment"? Are social work educators encouraging all students to commit themselves to public welfare work for at least two years? Are students encouraged to advocate for all services, public and private, to commit themselves to serve at least a certain percentage of poverty-level constituents? (See chapter 4.)

Another area to be considered is that of practice itself, and the questionable involvements and activities of professional practitioners. To what extent do services and service providers, during or after work hours, respond to the needs of the poor? Do agencies have a means of offering services for a certain percentage or number of low income/poor clients? Do practitioners spend at least some hours engaging in activities to benefit the poor? Finally, what efforts are being made by academic programs and service agencies to join in concerted efforts to identify and respond to the poor today?

The Public Welfare System

A manpower study conducted in the 1960s revealed that over 78 percent of social workers in public welfare had little or no preparation for their jobs.[5] As a result of this study the National Association of Social Workers (NASW) and the Council on Social Work Education (CSWE) agreed to accept baccalaureate social workers from accredited educational programs as entry level professionals. It was their intent that the B.S.W.'s would fill positions in public welfare, thus providing the profession a way to demonstrate and sustain its commitment to serving the poor. Few B.S.W. programs and practitioners, however, are in fact preparing for, or entering, public welfare services. Graduates of B.S.W. programs move quickly into M.S.W. programs or into private services.[6]

Questions to be considered, therefore, include: How do social workers gain an understanding of, and commitment to, the inherent values and purposes of the profession? How can they see the need and hear the call for them to carry on the mission of the profession, particularly through service in public welfare? And how can advanced practitioners realize that they cannot just pass the torch on to the beginning workers?

The curriculum of a professional social work education program is presented through classwork and field education by teachers and field instructors. At a recent meeting of social work educators and field instructors from accredited M.S.W. and B.S.W. programs,[7] a questionnaire was distributed asking:

1. As a social work teacher or field instructor, to what extent do you think you should foster in students a commitment to serving the materially poor?
2. To what extent would you say that you are currently serving the materially poor?
3. To what extent do you try to encourage students to work in public social services?
4. What are some examples of creative ways in which social workers in unrelated job locations (not serving the materially poor) could serve the poor today?

In response to the first question, 83 percent of the classroom and field instructors indicated that a commitment to serving the materially poor should be fostered in students. Seventy percent said that they themselves were currently serving the poor to some degree. Only 66 percent said that they strongly encouraged students to go into public social services to any large or great extent. No one suggested that students were encouraged to make a commitment to work in public welfare for at least a few years. Numerous examples were given of ways that social work educators and field instructors serve the poor today. These examples included:

a. Volunteering time to work with children in poverty areas (Big Brothers and Big Sisters, for example).
b. Developing satellite non-profit centers.
c. Introducing a sliding scale in one's agency.
d. Lobbying, giving testimony before legislative bodies.
e. Volunteering to work in shelters, food pantries, clothing closets, meals-on-wheels, pregnant teenage programs, helplines.
f. Providing in-service training to agencies about local dynamics of "the poor."

g. Establishing support groups.
h. Arranging speaking engagements to stimulate public concern.
i. Coordinating volunteer programs.
j. Taking leadership roles in politics.
k. Teaching families how to live in public housing.
l. Enhancing knowledge of human rights and services.
m. Developing a resource guide for the materially poor to find assistance.
n. Serving on "Friends of Black Children Councils."
o. Supporting social legislation benefiting the poor.
p. Serving as foster parents, refugee sponsors, or tutors to coach in low-income areas.
q. Providing transportation for the elderly.

Similar questions were asked of educators and practitioners from other service professions. In comparing the responses of teachers and field instructors from social work with those of other disciplines, a clear distinction became apparent in the extent of social workers' dedication and commitment to serve the poor. Although social work educators and practitioners did not indicate strong efforts to direct students into public social services, they did express a recognition of the need to foster their students' commitment to the poor, and they described numerous ways in which they themselves currently serve the poor. Most of the identified efforts were individual. Examples did not include major efforts by agencies and schools in collaboration with each other. The results indicated a continuance of the basic commitment to the poor, but a weakening of commitment to public welfare service. Since the majority of the constituents receiving public welfare are poor, there is an obvious need for further study and creative methods to promote commitment in this area.

The Curriculum

At the roots of social work practice is a steadfast sensitivity to the impact of society, or "the environment," on the development of the person and the family. As stated in previous chapters, social workers have recognized the social influences on behavior since the inception of the profession. The essence of social work has been its dual focus on both person and environment, although some social work schools or graduates focus primarily on the person or on a smaller system, such as the family.

It is apparent that a social worker must be able to deal with both individuals and environments when seeking causes and possible solutions to the problems or unmet needs of the poor. Practitioners working with low-income families are often called upon to demonstrate knowledge and skills in the areas of social development and social rights. For the professional working with such populations as those experiencing deprivation or discrimination, the most effective interventions often include 1) development of programs or policies, and 2) organization of depressed populations itself. In organizing those directly experiencing the problem or need, a worker is a "messenger of hope" (Keith-Lucas, chapter 4, p. 97) who helps to build their sense of self-worth, and provide them with opportunities for empowerment.

The question may be asked, do students who study social work in the classroom or in the field learn to enhance social rights or to promote social development? More specifically, to what extent is the foundation or advanced curriculum in social work programs applicable to work in the areas of social rights and social development?

All social work programs begin with a foundation curriculum that addresses the profession's basic values, knowledge, and skills. Content on social rights and social development may be included in this foundation curriculum. Considering the three major areas of values, knowledge, and skills, instructional opportunities could include the following:

I. Values

The two foundation values are often cited as:

1. The dignity and worth of every person.
2. The value of a democratic, caring society.[8]

As these values are addressed in the curriculum, special attention can be given to the rights of every person and every group of persons, because all are valuable human beings. The word "democratic" in the second foundation value refers to the principle that individual members of the society should participate in its power and planning. As this is explained, references can be made to social rights and to recognition that a "caring society" would foster the social development of the less fortunate. "Social development" can be explained as both a goal and a process involving a particular group of people in the development of just distribution of their society's resources and opportunities.

II. *Knowledge*

In the list of foundation theories studies in a social work curriculum, *knowledge* includes theories regarding individual, group, and environmental growth and development. Students also study social policy and community resources as part of their knowledge base. There is much opportunity to consider what may prevent individuals or groups from developing and becoming self-sufficient in all these content areas. Human rights, as well as the need to develop human potential, can be stressed.

III. *Skills*

Several skills are taught in foundation practice courses, and a pervasive theme of all such courses is the goal of enabling people to help themselves. When teaching the art of selecting appropriate skills, students learn first to clearly articulate their goals. Goals and skills are studied with a focus on how to move in a relationship from enabling to empowerment, from collaboration to independence, from professional leadership and consumer participation to citizen leadership and community organization, from helping the needy to responding to the rights of the needy, and from maintenance to prevention. Attention must be given to the goals of social development and social rights and to the skills necessary to achieve these goals.

The curriculum manual on *International Development Content in the Social Work Curriculum*, (which is currently being written under a matching grant of the National Association of Social Workers and the U.S. Agency for International

179

Development), offers additional content of extreme relevance for understanding and working with the poor both nationally and internationally.[9]

Generalist and Advanced Curriculum

In most first-year masters' programs, students are introduced to general practice, as discussed by Billups (chapter 6), utilizing a systems perspective and a problem-solving process to study the foundation of practice. The system's perspective encourages students to view individuals in the context of the various systems that directly influence their social and economic development. This problem-solving process is often described as consisting of six stages: 1) engagement, 2) data collection, 3) assessment, 4) intervention, 5) evaluation, and 6) termination. This practice model is particularly applicable to work with multiple problem systems in poor rural or urban areas.[10]

It is a process that clearly calls for co-planning (chapter 4) and it serves as a suitable model for quiet radicalism (chapter 6). In master's degree programs, the curriculum moves toward advanced areas of concentration. Graduate programs may be needed to make special efforts to help students see how their concentrations apply to the needs of low-income populations.

Agency-School Collaborations

There are several ways in which schools of social work and social service agencies could unite to mobilize resources and make a difference in the lives of today's poor. Although individual efforts are important, the complexity and pathology of poverty in America often call for major changes and developments through the extensive, unified efforts of many individuals and organizations.

In the remainder of this chapter, two examples demonstrate how social work educational programs and social service agencies joined to demonstrate their commitment to serving the poor. Both examples continue in eastern North Carolina, an area consisting of forty-one coastal plain counties. The area includes 45 percent of the state's land and 32 percent of its population. Eastern North Carolina is 56 percent rural. Although only 11.6 percent of North Carolina families are categorized as poor, 48.3 percent of these families live in the eastern region.[11]

Farm Community in Crisis

The School of Social Work at East Carolina University established a working relationship with an organized group of farmers called the People of the Land, located in a low-income rural community in eastern North Carolina. Although most rural people are unaccustomed to seeking help from universities (except through the extension agencies of predominantly land-grant colleges) the liaisons that made this possible were a local church and a private, religiously oriented family agency in a neighboring town. The family agency had been contacted for assistance by the pastor of this farm community church. He explained that he was aware of at least sixteen suicides or attempted suicides within one year in the farm community. He described the community as "in crisis," due to financial constraints and pressures from government agencies. The pastor also identified strong increases in family violence and alcohol abuse as growing community problems. The family agency had insufficient resources to meet the apparent extensive needs of this area. The director of the agency encouraged the pastor to contact the school of social work of the leading university in the eastern area of the state for assistance.

The Process

During the engagement stage of this work with the farm community, university faculty visited officers of the farm organization, the pastor of the church, the director of the family agency, and a representative of the local agricultural extension service. Although farmers in the area trusted their pastor and worked with him to develop their organization, there was initially in the farm community a strong sense of mistrust of the university, this decreased as contacts continued. At one point representatives of the university and of the family agency met with all members (approximately a hundred) of the People of the Land organization. Through such meetings farmers recognized that the university represented a vast resource, and that their rural community had a vast need. Efforts to articulate their differences led to co-planning and to designed interventions appropriate for the school as well as for the organization. The organization's representatives said that they clearly saw 1) a need for services for their families at this time, and 2) a need to help the general public become more aware of the plight of the poor in farm communities.

The Outcome

The school of social work worked with the farm community in ways which included 1) the writing of a grant to set up an area research and service center, to be owned by the farmers' organization, and 2) the establishment of a field unit where students could practice in the community under professional supervision by the family service agency, to provide the services and opportunities identified as needed by the community. The grant request was denied, but the family service agency was able to find funding to provide for a half-time M.S.W. social worker to work out of the church in the farm community. The School responded by placing students from the B.S.W. and M.S.W. programs to work under the supervision of the family service agency worker. The services offered from the church include youth groups, drug and alcohol counseling, individual and family counseling, and ongoing support for the farmer's organization. The field unit in this area is ongoing, and there appears to be increased stabilization throughout the community.

Eastern North Carolina Poverty Committee

In 1986 representatives from various disciplines at East Carolina University joined local agencies and organizations to study the reality of poverty in eastern North Carolina, and to take collective action in response to this growing problem. This effort began when the director of the Social Service Department of Fayetteville, North Carolina, and the dean of the School of Social Work at East Carolina University attended a state-wide meeting in Greensboro, North Carolina, to consider the question, "Do we have poverty in North Carolina?" The meeting was called by the Human Services Institute (later called "The Poverty Project") in the spring of 1986. It became apparent to the two eastern representatives that the participants knew little about the poverty of the rural east. In an effort to obtain information to substantiate the reality of that poverty, the group decided at the meeting to undertake separate studies of poverty in 1) western, 2) central, and 3) eastern North Carolina. Their task was to answer the question and to find strategies for responding to the needs of the poor in the state.

At the state-wide meeting, the two participants from the east decided to form an Eastern North Carolina Poverty Committee. They identified and contacted twenty-five individuals, representing regional legislators, educators, agency administrators, church representatives, and leaders of low-income communities, and invited them to a formation meeting. After much discussion and debate, twenty of those invited committed themselves to serve on a voluntary basis for three years. The goals of the Committee were identified:

1. To study the poor in eastern North Carolina today;
2. To identify causes and issues with an impact on the poor;
3. To identify human resources or services available to the poor;
4. To identify gaps or unmet needs in services for the poor;
5. To recommend models to meet the needs of the poor today.

More specifically, the committee set itself three goals:

1. To prepare a database;
2. To plan for educating the public;
3. To engage in political action to improve human services for the poor.

Definitions

Major attention was given initially to defining the meaning of the terms "poverty," "eastern North Carolina," and the "Eastern North Carolina Poverty Committee." The definition of poverty agreed upon by the Committee was an income below

$11,650 for a family of four. This definition was taken from
The Federal Register, U.S. Department of Health and Human
Services, "Annual Update of the Poverty Income Guidelines,"
dated 12 February 1988. Eastern North Carolina was identified
as the forty-one counties in North Carolina referred to as "the
east" by legislators and the state university system. The Committee itself was made up of five directors of county departments of social services, the deans of the Schools of Education
and of Social Work at East Carolina University, a state representative, a director of the local chamber of commerce, a director
of the local ministerial association, a director of a hospital social
service department, the president of the People of the Land, a
director of the local Council on Aging, a graduate student,
additional faculty members, practitioners from various service-
related areas, and community representatives.

In looking at the "poor" population, it became clear that
poverty was not just a matter of low incomes. Poverty was in
fact a systemic pathology, made up of many symptoms and
causal factors. The committee identified seven basic systems
which they called "the faces of poverty." These primary systems were 1) education, 2) health, 3) housing, 4) transportation,
5) industry and employment, 6) public social services, and 7)
private social services. The committee split into subcommittees to study each identified "face."

The Study

Data was collected from numerous sources. Local, state, and national studies were utilized. Subcommittees conducted their
own regional studies to obtain information when they were unable to find existing relevant data. In addition to ongoing subcommittee meetings, the Committee as a whole met monthly.
Throughout the first year, subcommittees reported their findings, and through dynamic discussion the group questioned, cri-
tiqued, and supported the efforts of each subgroup. Strong inter-
relationships among the various faces of poverty were quickly
recognized. For example, health problems increased when families had no transportation to medical appointments. Poor housing conditions often led to health problems.

After much collection and sharing of information, members

of the Committee considered how to pull their findings together and into a report. A format was agreed upon for each subcommittee. Each "face" report would contain the topical headings 1) Problem, 2) Services, and 3) Recommendations. The report would consist of an overview, definitions, subcommittee purpose, and a summary of each of the seven faces of poverty under the three topical headings. The report concluded with an appeal for all citizens to become aware and active in a concerted effort to deal with the problem of poverty.

The Report Release

The original organization that called the first meeting on the question of poverty in North Carolina grew into the North Carolina Poverty Project. This organization, located in central North Carolina, continues to observe and support the efforts of the Eastern North Carolina Poverty Committee. Through a grant they provided money to publish the report of the Committee. The first printing of the report, "Poverty in the East," was ready in December 1988.[12] The Committee released the report at two open hearings in different sections of eastern North Carolina. Both hearings were well attended by legislators, representatives of news media, human service personnel, and interested citizens. To the surprise of the Committee, at least twelve newspapers and three TV stations followed up with lead articles or presentations on the study findings. The Committee received hundreds of contacts from individuals and groups asking for copies of the report. Many of those who called said that it was the first time they had seen a concise, documented study of eastern North Carolina. Many wanted to use the report to support requests for assistance in various areas and programs. In addition, members of the Committee were invited to make presentations to various local and regional groups. Throughout its third year, the Committee's members met monthly and made presentations to groups. The Office of Peace and Justice of the Catholic Archdiocese of Raleigh expressed very strong support of the Committee's efforts, and demonstrated its support by donating $1,000 for a second printing of the report. Requests for copies of the report continued to be received by the Committee.

Positive effects appeared as a result of the report and the Committee's efforts. Increased funding was found for preschool programs, disadvantaged children programs, and enhanced transportation in rural areas. Local groups established committees to conduct similar studies in their counties or local areas. The caucus of the eastern state legislators met and welcomed the Committee's presentation. They agreed to have a subcommittee of their caucus work with members of the Committee to continue to identify and respond to poverty in the east.

For those who have served on the Committee, it has been a very exciting experience. The group is obviously a model for groups in other areas facing the problem of poverty. Apparently what was needed was an opportunity for individuals to unite to follow their consciences and their "moral vision" (Siporin, in Reamer's chapter 2). They made a commitment not to expect a quick remedy to solve the problem of poverty, but to persevere in hearing and responding to the cry of the poor.[13]

Summary

Social workers must recall their purpose and find creative ways to respond to their calling. Social work educators and practitioners can demonstrate their commitment to serving the poor today in three key areas: 1) public welfare service, 2) curriculum in professional programs, and 3) collaboration between social service agencies and professional schools. A B.S.W. or M.S.W. curriculum can reflect sensitivity to the needs of the poor through appropriate content and experiences for students. Individual social work educators and practitioners have become actively involved with the poor, and model their professional commitment for students. Finally, social service agencies and social work programs can join with people in poverty to make a difference in poverty-stricken communities or regions.

One key point is the need for social work educational programs, particularly at the baccalaureate level, to keep the profession focused on its historical moral mission and on its contemporary ethical responsibility to serve the poor. Such programs must also stress the recognized interdependence between the social work profession and the public welfare institution, and the value of their concerted commitment to respond to their call and mission through collaborative service.

In conclusion, social workers are still needed to confront the many faces of poverty and to respond to their calling. The primary face is that of a *child*, and the cry of the child is, in fact, the *call* of the poor today.

Notes

1. Commission on Social Work Practice, NASW, "Working Definition of Social Work Practice," quoted in Harriet M. Bartlett, "Toward Clarification and Improvement of Social Work Practice," *Social Work* 3 (April 1968):5–8.

2. Thomas Walz, "The Mission of Social Work Revisited: An Agenda for the 1990s," William R. Hodson Lecture, quoted in "The Public Social Services: The Social Work Role." *School of Social Work Alumni Report* (Minneapolis: University of Minnesota, 1989), 1.

3. Timothy Smeeding, Barbara Torrey, and Martin Rein, "Patterns of Income and Poverty: The Economic Status of Children and the Elderly in Eight Countries," in John Palmer and Barbara Torrey, eds., *The Vulnerable* (Washington, D.C.: The Urban Institute Press, 1988), 89–119.

4. National Association of Social Workers, Inc., *Code of Ethics of the National Association of Social Workers*, NASW Policy Statements 1 (1980), 9.

5. "Report of the Ad-Hoc Committee on Public Welfare to the Secretary of Health, Education, and Welfare—September, 1961," in *Hearings on H.R./10032, Public Welfare Amendments of 1962*, 78).

6. North Carolina Association of County Directors of Social Services, *Personnel Committee Report and Survey* (Onslow County, N.C.: North Carolina Association of County Social Services, December 1988).

7. Orientation Meeting, East Carolina University School of Social Work, August 1989.

8. Maria O'Neil McMahon, *The General Method of Social Work Practice: A Problem-Solving Approach*, 2nd ed. (Englewood Cliffs, N.J.: Prentice-Hall, 1990), 11.

9. Lyme Healy, "Introductory International Development Content in the Social Work Curriculum" (under review, Silver Spring, Md.: National Association of Social Workers, 1990).

10. McMahon, *The General Method of Social Work Practice: A Problem-Solving Approach*, 339, 344.

11. Rural Education Institute, School of Education, East Carolina University, *Eastern North Carolina: An Education Atlas* (Greenville, N.C.: Rural Education Institute, 1986).

12. Eastern North Carolina Poverty Committee, *Poverty in the East* (Greensboro, N.C.: North Carolina Poverty Project, 1988–1990).

13. From Psalm 34.

About the Contributors

James O. Billups received all of his degrees in social work—a B.S. from West Virginia University, an M.S.S.A. from Western Reserve University (Cleveland), and a D.S.W. from Washington University (St. Louis). He is at present on the faculty of the College of Social Work, The Ohio State University, where he is Chair of the Social Work Practice Teaching Unit. His social work practice experience has included military social work, youth work administration and consultation, and community planning. He has published in *The Journal of Education for Social Work, Social Development Issues, Social Work: Theory Into Practice, Social Work Research and Abstracts*, and *International Social Work*. He is President of the Inter-University Consortium for International Social Development.

Elizabeth D. Hutchinson received a B.A. in sociology from Maryville College, an M.S.W. from Washington University (St. Louis), and a Ph.D. in Social Welfare from the State University of New York at Albany. Currently she is on the faculty of the School of Social Work at Virginia Commonwealth University, where she serves as a faculty fellow on the Substance Abuse Curriculum Implementation Project. Her social work practice experience includes positions in health care, aging, mental health, and child welfare; at present, she is a volunteer group facilitator for Parents Anonymous in the Richmond City Jail. She has published in the areas of authority, child welfare, and homelessness. She was awarded the 1990 Frank R. Breul Memorial Prize for her article "Use of Authority in Direct Social Work Practice with Mandated Clients," which appeared in the December 1987 issue of *Social Service Review*.

Alan Keith-Lucas holds a B.A. and M.A. in English literature from Cambridge University, an M.Sc. in social work from Western Reserve University and a Ph.D. in political science from Duke University. For many years he served on the faculty of the School of Social Work at the University of North Carolina, where he is now Alumni Distinguished Professor Emeritus. He is recognized as an international expert in the field of institutional child care. He has published extensively on social work values and ethics; some of his more influential works are *Decisions About People in Need* (1957), *Giving and Taking Help* (1972), and entries on social work ethics in both the 1971 and 1977 volumes of the *Encyclopedia of Social Work*. He has recently published two books: *Essays From More Than Fifty Years in Social Work* and *The Poor You Have With You Always*. He is currently a board member of the North American Association of Christians in Social Work.

Beverly B. Koerin earned a B.S. in social science and an M.S.W. from Virginia Commonwealth University, and a Ph.D. in sociology from the University of Virginia. Since 1979 she has been on the faculty of Virginia Commonwealth University, where she is currently Associate Professor and Acting Associate Dean. Prior to coming to VCU, Dr. Koerin was an assistant professor of sociology at Randolph-Macon College. She has practiced direct social work in local, regional, and state departments of social services in Virginia. She has published in the areas of family and child welfare, women's history and policy issues, and administration in higher education and social work education.

Maria O'Neil McMahon holds a B.A. in English and mathematics from St. Joseph College, and an M.S.W. and D.S.W. from Catholic University. She has studied advanced social work practice at Smith College and is currently Professor and dean at East Carolina University. Her direct social work practice experience includes six years as a child and family therapist and supervisor at Highland Heights Residential Treatment Center in New Haven, Connecticut. She has published in the areas of child welfare, social work education, and family functioning. A second edition of her book *The General Method of Social Work Practice* has recently been published.

Wilma Peebles-Wilkins received a B.A. in sociology from North Carolina State University, an M.S.S.A. from Case Western Reserve University, and a Ph.D. in social foundations of education from the University of North Carolina. She is Associate Dean for Academic Affairs, School of Social Work, Boston University. She was previously on the faculty at North Carolina State University and Eastern Kentucky University. Her practice experience includes clinical social work, day care consultation, and child welfare work. Her publications focus on services to families and children, curriculum development, and social welfare history.

Philip R. Popple holds a B.S. from North Texas State University, and an M.S.W. and Ph.D. from Washington University (St. Louis). He is currently Associate Professor and Department Head, Department of Sociology, Anthropology, and Social Work at Auburn University. He has direct practice experience as a child welfare worker, public welfare planner, and as a child welfare trainer, curriculum developer, and training administrator. He has published in the areas of sociology of social work and social welfare history and is coauthor of a recently published textbook, *Social Work, Social Welfare, and American Society.*

Frederic G. Reamer holds a Ph.D. in social work from the University of Chicago. He is currently a Professor in the graduate program of the School of Social Work at Rhode Island College, and Commissioner of the Rhode Island Housing and Mortgage Finance Corporation. He has direct practice experience in a variety of criminal justice, mental health, and affordable housing agencies. He recently served as a senior policy advisor to the Governor of Rhode Island. Dr. Reamer is the author of *Ethical Dilemmas in Social Service,* coauthor of *Rehabilitating Juvenile Justice,* and editor of *AIDS and Ethics.* He is the editor-in-chief of the *Journal of Social Work Education.*

P. Nelson Reid received an A.B. in sociology and anthropology and an M.S.W. from the University of North Carolina, then earned a Ph.D. from The Ohio State University. He is currently Professor of Social Work at North Carolina State University.

He has direct practice experience in community organization and regional development. He has published articles on the social work profession, welfare reform, income redistribution, conservative perspectives on social welfare, and the social functions of social welfare. He has published general interest pieces in news magazines such as *The New Republic* as well as contributed to professional journals such as *Social Work, Journal of Social Work Education, Social Service Review,* and the *CATO Journal.*

Max Siporin holds an M.S.S.W. from Columbia University and a D.S.W. from the University of Pittsburgh. He is currently Professor Emeritus in the School of Social Welfare at the State University of New York at Albany. Prior to coming to Albany in 1969, Siporin taught at the University of Kansas, Tulane University, and the University of Maryland. He has direct practice experience as a private practitioner in marriage and family therapy and is approved as a supervisor by the American Association of Marriage and Family Therapists. He has also worked as a medical and psychiatric social worker and family counselor with the Veterans Administration. He is the author of many papers on clinical practice and on social work philosophy and morality. In 1975 he published *An Introduction to Social Work Practice,* one of the few texts with a chapter on philosophy and practice. He is currently working on a book dealing with the art of social work practice.

Index

Index

Index